George S. Sylvester Counts:

Educator for a New Age

Edited by Lawrence J. Dennis and William Edward Eaton

Southern Illinois University Press
Carbondale and Edwardsville
Feffer & Simons, Inc. : London and Amsterdam

Extracts used in this text as taken with permission from:

The book *Secondary Education and Industrialism* by George S. Counts
Copyright 1929 by the President and Fellows of Harvard College, Harvard University Press

The book *A Call to the Teachers of the Nation* by George S. Counts (The Progressive Education Association)
Copyright 1933 by John Day Co.
Permission granted by The John Dewey Society

The book *The Social Foundations of Education* by George S. Counts (Report of the Commission on the Social Studies, Part IX).
Copyright 1934, 1952 by Charles Scribner's Sons

The book *The Prospects of American Democracy* by George S. Counts (John Day Co.)
Copyright 1938 by George S. Counts
Harper & Row, Publishers, Inc.

The book *Education and the Promise of America* by George S. Counts
Copyright 1945 by the Macmillan Publishing Co., Inc.
Permission granted by Kappa Delta Pi

The book *Education and American Civilization* by George S. Counts
Copyright 1952 by Teachers College Press, Columbia University
Reprinted 1973 by Greenwood Press

The book *Education and the Foundations of Human Freedom* by George S. Counts
Copyright © 1963 by the University of Pittsburgh Press

Library of Congress Cataloging in Publication Data

Counts, George Sylvester, 1889-1974.
    George S. Counts, educator for a new age.

    Bibliography: p.
    Includes index.
    1. Counts, George Sylvester, 1889-1974. 2. Education—United States—History. 3. National characteristics, American. 4. United States—Civilization—20th century. I. Dennis, Lawrence J. II. Eaton, William Edward, 1943-   III. Title.
LB885.C66 1980   370'.092'4   79-28182
ISBN 0-8093-0954-8

Contents

Preface

At the time of George Counts's death, November 10, 1974, most of his writings were out of print, and they have remained so. They are available, of course, in university libraries, where they are usually well-worn and much-marked—an indication of their extensive use in years past. We hope that in future years these books will be reissued, for Counts, almost more than any of his contemporaries, brought into focus some fundamental educational problems that are of a continuing nature.

In the following pages we concern ourselves not with the whole body of Counts's work, but with that portion of it, the largest portion by far, that deals with culture and with schooling and the relationship between them. In this area five main themes recur over and over: (1) a view of national character shaped both by the history of the American people and by the topography of the land; (2) an examination of the nature of the social forces that affect formal schooling; (3) a conviction that his life spanned the great watershed of human history as civilization moved from an agrarian to an industrial age; (4) a faith that the twentieth century stands witness to the struggle between totalitarianism in several forms and democracy in imperfect forms; and (5) a belief that teachers can make a small but appreciable difference in shaping the course of the future. Sometimes, indeed, they are expressed in almost identical words, especially in later talks and articles. These five themes represent the main strands of Counts's thought. For this reason, we present extracts which, we hope, will violate neither his thoughts nor his purposes. If these extracts prompt readers to return to Counts's complete writings, so much the better, for those who do read the complete works will be rewarded with a clearer realization of the relationship of culture to education, with a greater understanding of the role of the teacher in today's society, and with a deeper appreciation of the responsibilities of the school in the preparation of young people to assume the obligations of citizenship.

In the main, the excerpts have been reprinted without deletion. The only omissions in the complete text, except for two lengthier ones in chapter 6, are those that make reference to earlier or later parts of the volumes in which they appear. In some cases it has been necessary to interpolate a word or a phrase, which is always contained in brackets. Paragraph headings have been removed to keep the style of this present book as uniform as possible. We have taken the excerpts from the first printing of each book, and Counts's bibliographic references have been updated and corrected. Spellings and diacritical markings have been modernized.

Readers will notice that the selections have not been arranged in chronological sequence. Counts did not, we maintain, significantly change his views during his mature years, that is from around 1928, except in one important regard. The exception is his view of the Soviet regime. It is not difficult to see that he was more kindly disposed to the Soviet Union up through the middle 1930s than he was later. This is not to suggest that he was ever blind to its limitations, but he certainly came to focus increasingly on its menace as time passed. But his Russian studies do not have a place in this volume.

The chronological checklist of the writings of Counts is as complete as we could make it at the time of going to press. A checklist is perforce always in process; some obvious gaps will result from lack of resources, of time, of instinct. No attempt has been made to list foreign editions or translations, of which there are several, nor to list subsequent printings of any of his books. Articles in newspapers are hard to unearth, except for those in the *New York Times,* but they tend to show a side of Counts, avid reader and student of current events that he was, that his more considered works do not.

Several of his writings were excerpted, printed in condensed form, or published in more than one place. The student will discover these, and, for others, the titles generally suggest the obvious. Reports of Counts's speeches or writings were quite numerous; these will not be found in the checklist, unless, of course, they were published verbatim and without editorial comment.

In preparing this manuscript for print the editors gratefully acknowledge the enthusiastic support of Dr. Harry G. Miller, Chairman of the Department of Educational Leadership at Southern Illinois University at Carbondale. We also thank those who have been generous in granting us permission to use materials, particularly Miss Martha Counts.

Lawrence J. Dennis
William Edward Eaton
Carbondale, Illinois
October 1979

George S. Counts

1 The Professional Life of George S. Counts

In 1913 George Counts entered graduate school at the University of Chicago. The University held great appeal for the young man from Kansas, who saw it as a bastion of liberal ideas and a center of open inquiry about great social issues. His original intention to study sociology was somewhat modified after a discussion with Charles Hubbard Judd, who was able to convince Counts that professional education needed fertile minds and that there would be no barrier to entertaining broad social issues as a student of pedagogy. Counts accepted this advice and began his studies under the direct supervision of Judd.[1]

It was an exciting era in which to study education; the favorable place and the opportunity of working with Judd made the whole experience good for Counts. The School of Education still carried the bloom of John Dewey and Francis W. Parker. Educators were engaged in the determined plan of developing a science of education, and Judd was one of the leading architects of this plan.

Charles H. Judd had already achieved distinction as a psychologist. After earning his A.B. from Wesleyan in 1894, he had traveled to Germany, like so many aspiring American academics, to pursue the doctorate at Leipzig. He returned to the States in 1896 to teach for two years at his alma mater before moving on to New York University as a professor of experimental psychology.[2] After a year at the University of Cincinnati, he accepted an instructorship at Yale in 1902 and became director of the psychological laboratory. In 1909 he was made director of the School of Education at Chicago.[3] His selection by Chicago was indicative of the national effort to make pedagogy more scientific.

When Counts first met Judd, the director had already moved from the posture of a rather strict laboratory psychologist to that of a social psychologist, and he permitted students to choose either sociology or psychology as a major concentration. Counts was the first to select the option of sociology. Later in his life, Counts used to recall that he was the first person ever to graduate from the University of Chicago with a doctorate in sociology of education. He always made this recollection with a wry grin since Judd denied that the degree was in anything other than educational psychology.

Counts was very busy as a graduate student. He managed to take every course offered in sociology and anthropology as well as courses in the School of Education. He was also Judd's graduate assistant. The latter task would have seemed formidable, for Judd managed the School of Education, stalked about the country conducting a variety of school surveys, continued to write a steady stream of books and articles, and contracted special research studies for the United States Bureau of Education.

Part of Counts's assistantship required him to help Judd prepare the research reports. In 1915 one such study, entitled *A Study of the Colleges and High Schools in the North Central Association*, was produced for the Bureau of Education. Judd wrote the section on colleges and Counts the section on high schools. Counts had, after all, worked as a high school teacher of mathematics and science and as a high school principal immediately after his graduation in 1911 from Baker College, now Baker University, located in Baldwin, Kansas. This research activity was of professional importance to George Counts, as it gave him a reputation as something of an expert on secondary education.

Counts completed his doctorate in 1916 and took his first job as head of the Department of Education at Delaware College at Newark, Delaware. He moved on to Harris Teachers College in St. Louis in 1918 and to the University of Washington in 1919. Frank Ellsworth Spaulding, when he became the first chairman at the newly formed Department of Education, brought Counts to Yale in 1920.[4] In 1926, Counts returned briefly to the University of

Chicago. In 1927, his long career at Teachers College, Columbia University, began.

Teachers College was in its zenith when George Counts was added to its formidable faculty: Paul Monroe, George Strayer, I. L. Kandel, Edward Reisner, Harold Rugg, William Heard Kilpatrick, and Edward Thorndike were among the list of luminaries. Counts himself, along with newer faculty like John Childs, Paul Mort, Jesse Newlon, and R. Freeman Butts, was to contribute greatly to the preeminence of the institution.

In 1925, Counts had been invited by Paul Monroe to join a survey team that examined the educational system of the Philippines. His early assignment at Teachers College would be in this emerging field of international education, and, as he told the story, by the time he arrived the world had already been divided up among the other scholars, leaving him no choice but to select the Soviet Union. As with everything else he undertook, George Counts approached the new assignment with intelligence and vigor and set into motion plans to visit Russia and to learn her language. Those of us who knew him still remember his spending time every morning reading the Soviet newspaper, *Pravda*, which he received by air mail from Moscow. By 1928, he was addressing the National Education Association on "The Educational Program of Soviet Russia," and he quickly established himself as an authority on Russian education and Russian society.

During the middle 1920s Counts's major efforts were still being directed to the secondary school. These later studies of the high school were a change from his earlier work, which had been influenced by the more empirical procedures of Judd that utilized survey and quantification techniques. Away from Judd, the studies done by Counts in the 1920s reflected more of his own inclination toward broadly based historical-cultural analyses.

In May 1929, he was invited to give the Inglis Lecture at Harvard University. The lecture series, which was instituted in 1925 honoring the distinguished career of Alexander Inglis—an expert on the American high school who had died the year before—was becoming a premier event. Shortly before the death of Inglis, Counts had talked with him about the relationship between the American secondary school and the process of industrialization. This became the theme of Counts's 1929 lecture. It is interesting to note that the 1928 Inglis Lecture had been given by Judd.[5]

George Counts was now drawing upon what he felt to be the essential historical lessons of America's past, and he turned to the writings of James Harvey Robinson and Charles A. Beard as he reflected upon the contours of the nation's history. He had planned, at one point in this early part of his career, to write a book entitled: "The Story of Human Progress." It was never completed because, as he said, H. G. Wells beat him to it with his *Outline of History*.[6] Counts must have had a lingering fondness for this early effort, for he saved the finished parts of the manuscript, most of it in long-hand on brittle, fading paper.

Counts viewed history as depicting the sweep of collective human experience from which one could draw usable generalizations about mankind, from which one could extract pattern and form, and from which one could glean the essence of human meaning and purpose. Such a view of the written past was certainly a grand view and not unromantic. His own preference for this inclusive view of history caused him to have only limited interest in the historical technicalities of finding one new datum or validating an assumed fact. Thus he was sometimes led to depreciate the daily labors of historical scholarship. His friend and associate, Charles A. Beard, advised him to make a distinction "between facts empirically established and aspirations deliberately chosen."[7] The latter fascinated Counts, and this predilection attracted him to historians like H. G. Wells and to commentators on national character such as Alexis de Tocqueville. Counts probably quoted de Tocqueville more than any other author.

With de Tocqueville, Counts believed that the strength of American institutions was rooted in a rather fundamental instinct for freedom among the people and in their inherent practical wisdom in creating democratic associations for the preservation of that freedom. But this vision was not without its countervailing force, for Counts believed that man's almost natural tendency toward freedom could be checked by forces of avarice, ambition, and power. The task of the historian then was to portray both the quest for freedom and the antithetical forces that opposed it so that we, as consumers of history, could use the past to interpret the present.

Counts seems to be further intellectually indebted to de Tocqueville for the interest in "national character." He believed that America's "natural endowment"—its climate, geography, topography, and location—had strongly influenced both the character of the people and the direction of social movement. In spite of the fact that Charles A. Beard told George Counts, in rather strong words, that the developments in cultural anthropology did not support the position that "national character" was occasioned in part by the geography of a nation,[8] Counts clung to the notion. It is an appealing one, of course, and common sense seems to indicate that it is an inescapable one. After all, do not the mountains and the prairies and the ocean white with foam have something to do with what we are? Counts thought so, anyway, and he made frequent and wistful references to his adolescent dream of becoming a trapper and living in close contact with the land and its seasons. It was a grand, if somewhat romanticised, portrayal, and he treated the vast differences not only of ethnic but also of regional background somewhat cavalierly.

Although in his depiction of history and national character Counts oversimplified and ironed out the rough edges, his panoramic view was not entirely invalid. Count's educational philosophy of reconstructionism was based on his views of history and national character; indeed, the philosophy makes no sense at all apart from these views, for Counts believed that educational practice essentially reflected the society of which it was a part. He stated emphatically that "education is always an expression of a particular society and culture at a particular time in history, unless it is imposed by force from without."[9] He recognized as important the fact that American soil had not been violated by the steps of invading armies. (That the American Indian might think differently did not really cross his mind.) Thus Counts's reconstructionism should not be viewed as Utopian, but rather as the recognition, the rediscovery, and the reevaluation of America's vital roots.

The change of the United States from an agricultural nation to an industrial nation struck Counts as being enormously important. This change was not one of degree, but one of kind. The industrial age heralded a *new* social order, but not one that was necessarily compatible with democracy. For with the rise of the industrial state had come financial oligopoly, irresponsible corporate power, and the contrived corruption of democratic institutions. Nineteenth-century political freedoms had been enhanced by a set of laws clearly postulated and generally understood as well as by a sense of morality tempered by formal religion and by grass roots institutions that sprang from informal cooperation. These freedoms were further enhanced by the realities of geographic vastness and the slowness of communication; thus the freedom of the individual had been in part guaranteed by natural checks against those who would own his soul. This was no longer the case in the twentieth century, however. The telegraph, the telephone, the railroad, the radio, the highways, and later the television had gathered people from scattered villages into a national community. This new national community could act as a positive force for the education of the masses, for the diffusion of culture, and for the prospect of human development; but it also offered a community now suddenly susceptible to the contagion of antidemocratic disease. The rise of the corporate state in Italy, the use of mass communication for the spread of propaganda in Germany, and the subversion of the schools for purposes of political indoctrination in both Italy and Germany were not overlooked by Counts as he drew frequently and fervently from this reservoir of example. Only more gradually did he come to see the Soviet system to be as insidious a threat as fascism.

The themes of history were portrayed by Counts in his book, *The American Road to Culture*, published in 1930. The book received first-page attention in the *New York Times Book Review* of July 27. In addition to the full treatment afforded by the lead review, Counts was photographed for the occasion and he stiffly stares at the reader through his wire-rimmed glasses. A bushy moustache and a cardboard collar round out the picture of the serious academic.[10]

Counts also used history in a personal way. He was not content simply to lay out history in large form; he tried also to place himself as a part of that large picture. The generalizations he clung to throughout his life had to be those that could include growing up on a farm in Kansas. To be truly important, the wisdom of the ages had to address his personal observations and experiences. The older he got, the more this seemed to be true. In his final teaching days at Southern Illinois University, he increasingly loved to sing in rather loud fashion the Methodist hymns of his boyhood and to recall the details of himself as a farm boy and a youthful trapper, not as a distinguished professor. The remembrances of his youth actualized the quintessence of western expansion, the purity of democratic institutions, and the transition of an agrarian nation to an industrial world power.

In 1929, George S. Counts began work as a member of the American Historical Association's Commission on the Social Studies. Among the sixteen people serving with him were A. C. Krey of the University of Minnesota as commission chairman, Charles E. Merriam of Chicago, and Charles A. Beard. Counts was appointed the commission's Director of Research in the summer of 1931 at the handsom salary of $15,000, of which one-fourth was to be paid by Teachers College.[11]

The American Historical Association had had a long interest in the teaching of history in the schools and had published its first report as early as 1898. The interest, however, was ongoing and actively supported by such distinguished historians as James Harvey Robinson, A. M. Schlesinger, and Charles Beard. The Commission, formed following the American Historical Association's Christmas meetings of 1925, was to look at a wide range of issues concerning the social sciences and schools and to publish their findings in several volumes. Funding for the organizational efforts of the commission was provided by the Commonwealth Fund and operational monies came from the Carnegie Corporation. The first volume by the commission was Beard's *A Charter for the Social Sciences*, published in 1932; work on subsequent volumes continued through 1937. Beard and Counts were co-authors of the summary volume, *Conclusions and Recommendations of the Commission*, which four members of the commission refused to sign.[12] The greatest thing that the commission did for Counts was to bring him into a closeworking relationship with Charles A. Beard and from this relationship a life-long friendship bloomed.

The years at Teachers College were busy ones for Counts. They were modulated by the intensity of a bustling New York City and the quietude of the recently purchased farm in Bucks County, Pennsylvania; by the organizational chores of a growing number of clubs, groups, and associations freely undertaken by Counts as differentiated from the more personal demands of scholarship; and by the disquieting success of national socialism in the fascist countries contrasted with the growing stagnation of the American economy.

Counts lived in an apartment just above the bookstore at Teachers College. From here it was but a short walk to the classrooms and library of the college. By traveling only a little farther one would find oneself in the middle of one of the world's largest cities. Seeing the lengthening lines of the unemployed and hearing the cries from the full range of political thought, it was easy to conclude that this was democracy's laboratory and that the experiment was in jeopardy.

In 1929, Counts took his most extensive tour of the Soviet Union. He made arrangements to ship a newly made Model A Ford complete with spare parts from Detroit to Leningrad. He arrived in the Soviet Union with a proficiency in the Russian language, with as complete a scholarly background as the existing books on the Soviet Union could then afford him, and with his insatiable curiosity to learn as much as he could about the nation, its institutions, its geography, and especially its people.

Counts logged over 6,000 miles in Russia, a great part of which was over terrain barely passable by automobile. He spoke, not just to the commissars and to party officials, but to the ordinary people. He studied the Soviet Union from the Kremlin ideology downward and from the soil of Mother Russia upward, grasping from somewhere between these extremes the essence of the revolution. It was the revolution that captured Counts's mental fancy. The officiousness of the Bolshevik bureaucracy, the heavy-handed propaganda, and the marshalling of the masses to build the industrial state under the new Five-Year Plan were certainly not ignored by Counts, nor was their importance lost to him. But these realities were secondary to the meaning that Counts felt the Russian revolution held for the common people. The revolution contained many messages that needed to be decoded so that all might know their contents—the death of despotic monarchy, the new reign of ideology, and a state with grand design were but three parts of a more complex cipher. One can sense Counts's excitement in a letter written from Moscow to his old teacher, Charles Judd: "There never was before such a vast sociological laboratory."[13]

The trip to the Soviet Union took Counts out of the United States for eight months. By the end of January 1930, he was back in New York City sporting a beard, that, with his brushed-back shock of red hair, made him look for all the world like Trotsky. His expertise on the Soviet Union, a topic that has probably fas-

cinated the American people as much as any other during the
twentieth century, earned him dozens of invitations to lunch, dinner, and discussion forums. He was also becoming "hot copy" for
the press as he called for improving relationships with the Soviet
Union at a time when the common American attitude was one of
suspicion toward the Russians. He was also calling for central
planning in the United States when such schemes were generally
thought to be socialistic and therefore anathema to our system of
free enterprise. If there is such a thing as a formula for making the
pages of the *New York Times* with regularity, it might be contained in two parts: (1) say something important, or (2) say something that people think is outrageous. Counts did both of these
throughout his career and "made the *Times*" with frequency.

On his return from Russia, Counts encountered the early effects of the depression, which weighed upon him intellectually.
The "slump," as those of a more optimistic view might term it,
seemed to accentuate all of the problems inherent in a capitalistic
democracy. It was a time of extremes: the tensions of rich versus
poor, autocratic versus democratic, and soft-hearted idealism versus hard-headed realism seemed to place everything else in juxta-
position and to create a bipolar world. Counts pondered this jum-
ble and, as was his wont, sought to discover the broad meaning of
the various events. What was required, thought Counts, was a different social structure, one not entirely new, but one already
grounded in the roots of the past: the United States Constitution,
the basic governmental organization, and the traditions of freedom would be sufficient. The economic forms would be different,
though; free enterprise would be displaced by a planned economy.
He called for the development of a socialistic society, for a form
of "democratic collectivism." He was gently chided by his friend
Charles Beard for using terms that were loaded with emotional
currency,[14] and "democratic collectivism" drops from Counts's
later writings and in its place he talks of "general planning," and
"general economic planning." But it is clear, nevertheless, that he
believed it was essential to develop some type of benevolently
planned society that would be in the best interests and general
welfare of all. Among the principal engineers of this reconstruction would be the teachers of the nation.

In April 1932, Counts addressed the Progressive Education
Association meeting in Baltimore. He chose as the title of his ad-

dress: "Dare Progressive Education Be Progressive?" In that speech he issued his stirring challenge to the teachers of the country to assume the leadership in the reconstruction. Even as we read the address today, we question whether Counts really believed that teachers were in a position to do as he suggested; and even if they were, *would* they. Though his later statement that it "was polemical," that it "was an arouser,"[15] does not carry much conviction, that Counts considered the challenge as a blueprint rather than a parlor game seems borne out by his activities of the period. He was deeply interested in civil rights, civil liberties, and the union movement, and he joined a number of organizations related to these concerns.

In 1934, Counts became the editor of a new educational periodical to be called the *Social Frontier*. He had been asked by "a group of radicals in education"[16] to undertake the editorship. Counts saw it as an opportunity to deal with educational matters from the perspectives that he and Charles Beard had already outlined in their report for the Commission for the Social Sciences, which was formally disbanded in December 1933. When asked by a *Times* reporter about the purposes of the new journal, Counts replied: "It will advocate the raising of American life from the level of the profit system, individualism and vested class interests to the plane of social motivation, collectivism, and classlessness. . . . It will oppose those elements which, under the guise of devotion to American ideals, would stabilize for all time the essentials of our business system and thus preserve them in the exercise of special privilege."[17]

The *Social Frontier* became a major vehicle for expressing the viewpoint of the social reconstructionists. Though the editor, editorial assistants, and most of the contributors were educationists, no one who read the journal leveled charges of pedagogical parochialism. The approach was broadly based, universal, and theoretical. Education was conceived as the entire process of enculturation and not simply as *schooling*. John Dewey was active as a contributing editor, and a quick perusal of the articles reveals important names and ideas from the full spectrum of American social thought in the 1930s. It was, in a sense, the *New Republic* for educators.

When Counts turned the editorial responsibilities of the *Social Frontier* over to George W. Hartmann in 1937, it was not out of a

sense of uninterest, but rather an instance of a fertile mind finding something new to occupy its full attention. In any case, he
had agreed from the outset to hold the position for three years. It
was at this time that Counts turned his energies to political in-
volvement; the first arena he chose was the teachers' union movement. He had joined Local #5 of the American Federation of
Teachers, the largest local in that national organization, in the
early 1930s. The local was an amalgam of both public school
teachers and university faculty. Later it would divide into two
separate locals, but in the mid-1930s it was caught in a tumultu-
ous struggle to find a compromise between diverse ideological and
practical factions. The meetings of Local #5 became the focal
points of argument between theoretical Marxists, Stalinists, practical unionists, socialists, and just about any other movement that
ended with an *ism*. By 1935 the leadership of the local had lost
control, and many of Counts's colleagues, like John Childs, had
withdrawn believing the organization to be effectively controlled
by communist elements inimical to the interests of the teaching
profession. Counts, however, retained his membership, not yet
fully realizing the ultimate ambitions of those on the far left.

By 1938 George S. Counts became aware of an organized con-
spiracy to prostitute the teachers' union to the goal of international communism. He was slow to arrive at this conclusion but
quick to commit his energies to what he hoped would be a solution. He ran for the presidency of the college section of the New
York local and was soundly beaten, but on account of his growing
fame as a scholar and educational leader, he was invited to stand
for the presidency of the American Federation of Teachers. He
won his first election in September of 1939 and served three con-
secutive terms as federation president. During his term two large
locals in New York City and another in Philadelphia were ex-
pelled for being communist controlled.[18]

The Union presidency was extremely time-consuming. Counts
records that he gave about one hundred and ten speeches during
his first term as union president. Long and tedious train trips to
American Federation of Teachers locals scattered all over the
country, unavoidable chicken dinners, and impromptu speeches
became a way of life. Not long after returning from his extensive
trip to the Soviet Union, Counts had hired Nucia Perlmutter as
translator, research assistant, and secretary. Miss Perlmutter, later

Mrs. Lodge, was instrumental in seeing that the trips were planned, that the university obligations were met, and that scholarship continued. She directed the student traffic in and out of his office at Teachers College, answered his mail, and monitored the mounting demands for him as lecturer or program participant.

Counts was now a national figure. He was the president of the second largest teacher group in the country, he was an established authority on Russia, he had high standing as a social commentator, and he was becoming recognized internationally as a perceptive educational thinker. He was constantly being berated by the conservative press for his interest in Russia, and, despite his demonstrable record of anti-Communist activities, he was still being denounced as a fellow traveler and called by his detractors "Red Russia's Apostle"[19] through the McCarthy era of the 1950s. He had also become an established political figure in the state of New York.

Counts's interest in national issues, his commitment to activism, and his growing interest in the labor movement led him to join the American Labor party. The American Labor Party was an officially recognized political party in the state of New York and ran candidates where it could, or coalesced to support regular Republican or Democratic Party candidates when an appropriate deal could be struck. Ideologically the party stood to the left of both traditional parties, although it had endorsed and supported Franklin D. Roosevelt throughout. In 1941, Counts accepted the American Labor party's nomination as a candidate from the borough of Manhattan to run for city council. The party, however, was already badly split between two camps usually described as the right wing and the left wing. Later in life, Counts like to relate that he had played left guard on his high school football team and left forward on the basketball team and that he had been on the left ever since. Even at the expense of destroying such a colorful description, it should be pointed out that in the struggle within the American Labor Party, Counts found himself on the right. And yet the story is still salvageable since the right wing of the American Labor party was, nonetheless, to the left of center.

The election was held in November of 1941. Despite support from leading figures in the American Civil Liberties Union, the Amalgamated Clothing Workers, and the International Ladies Garment Workers Union, Counts lost badly. Interestingly, one of the left-wing candidates of the American Labor party won handily, a young minister from Harlem just beginning his political career— Adam Clayton Powell, Jr.[20] Counts would grow to appreciate this defeat since it added interesting material for the old man of later years to chortle about as he gasped and choked over the vodka he was not supposed to be drinking.

In 1942, Counts was elected State Chairman of the American Labor party. The party platform of 1942 was rather lengthy, but it included strong planks for organized labor and protections for consumers; it urged greater taxes on corporations, and opposed cuts in educational expenditures.[21]

By 1944, the schism within the party had widened to a gulf and the party split. The so-called left wing continued to use the name of the American Labor party while the so-called right wing became the American Liberal party, with Counts at the helm. He continued to serve as an important official of the party through the 1950s.

The culmination of this earlier political activity came in August of 1952 when Counts was nominated by the Liberal party as a candidate for the United States Senate. There were initially a good half dozen candidates for the job, but after the usual hoopla and tumult, four emerged: Irving M. Ives, the Republican incumbent; John Cashmore, the Democratic challenger; Counts; and Corliss Lamont of the American Labor party.[22]

Ives, who had defeated former governor Herbert H. Lehman in the first election, would not be easy to defeat in a presidential year that would have millions of Americans flocking to the polls to vote for General Eisenhower. Ives also had a reputation as a liberal Republican with an established voting record in favor of Negro rights. Counts, holding no illusions about the inevitable outcome, had tried to encourage Cashmore to withdraw, promising that he would do likewise and that a Democratic-Liberal coalition could then be formed, drafting Averell Harriman as the coalition candidate. Cashmore did not accept these terms, so Counts remained in the race.

When the votes were counted that November night, Ives was returned to office with nearly four million votes. Cashmore garnered about two and one-half million votes, Counts claimed around half a million, with Lamont settling for close to one hundred thousand. The election gave Counts the opportunity to speak both personally and through the media to thousands of people on a variety of issues.[23]

By 1950, George S. Counts had witnessed and participated in over one-half century of American life. It was a good time to reflect on those fifty-plus years and he did just that. The nation had survived two world wars, a major depression, and an entire battery of cultural and political divisions. But despite dire predictions, the country stood firm in 1950 and made those who might have thought about such things wonder why. Counts did wonder. In 1952, he published his *Education and American Civilization*, which he always considered his best work. He was now nearing the end of his career at Teachers College. During these final four years, he stayed busy directing the theses of a group of students who are eminent today in American education and in education throughout the world. He continued to teach to classes that were quickly filled and to respond to the large number of invitations to speak here and there. In 1954, Teachers College awarded him a medal for distinguished service. Though the spectre of compulsory retirement awaited him in 1955, he did not succumb to the temptation to "gear down"; he continued to rail at the enemies of civil liberties and at the champions of political and economic privilege. But 1955 did come, and Counts was officially retired. While accepting the mandate with a public stoicism, he was personally hurt at being torn from his academic position during what he thought could have been some of his most productive years.

The shock lifted after a time, and Counts was faced with a decision: retire to the Bucks County farm to raise azaleas and wait for the visits of the grandchildren, as he purposed, or begin a new career. The decision was really only theoretical, and those who knew George Counts were not surprised when he chose to continue to travel, to lecture, and to teach. He went to Brazil in 1957 for a lecture series, joined the faculty at the University of Pittsburgh in 1959, and the faculty at Michigan State in 1960. In 1961, he was invited to join the faculty of Southern Illinois University at Carbondale. When he agreed, he was sent the standard teaching contract and an application to fill out. Height, five feet, eleven inches; weight, 170 pounds; state of health, good; physical defects, none; specialization, the social foundations.[24]

Counts arrived in Carbondale, Illinois in 1962. He taught courses renamed at his suggestion to "Education and Social

Forces," "Soviet Education," and "The Twentieth Century and
Education." At Southern, he joined a group of distinguished visit-
ing professors that included his old friends and colleagues, John
Childs and George Axtelle. He became the autocrat of the coffee
pot and the gadfly of the informal discussion. He earned the love
of students and faculty and gained the reputation as the world's
best storyteller and the world's worst automobile driver. In 1971,
he left teaching for the final time to live in a retirement home.
One of his last acts in Carbondale was to sell the home he had
built to the dean of Southern Illinois University's School of Engineering, Tom Jefferson. "I'm proud," he would say, "to know
that my home was good enough for Thomas Jefferson."

It is perhaps a risky business to attempt an assessment of
Counts's importance in the development of educational thought
in America. He had neither the philosophic reach of Dewey, nor
the practical influence of Cubberley; neither the theoretical effect
of Thorndike, nor the teaching impact of Kilpatrick. Theodore
Sizer calls Counts "a stimulating visionary," whose "ideas, although applauded by many teachers, were never put into practice."[25] But Sizer's assessment is incorrect, because Counts's ideas
were not narrowly pedagogical. He had almost nothing to say
about classroom management, teaching methodology, the day-to-
day problems that confront teachers, nothing about the particu-
larities of primary, elementary, secondary, and higher education,
and only a little about curriculum, and still less concerning the
administration of the schools. He assumed, probably correctly,
that problems in these areas were symptoms of a far larger problem—the relationship between schools and society, a relationship
that was in danger of becoming, if it was not already, out of kilter.

Counts recognized and asserted over and over again that the
schools only reflect the society of which they are a part. But in a
free, fluid, democratic society, the schools are in a position (indeed, they have the responsibility) to extrapolate the "good" and
to discard the "bad." What they extrapolate and discard should
be up to the teachers—and it is perhaps worthy of note that he
expressly talks about the teachers and their responsibilities with
respect to educational planning, rather than about administrators
or boards of education. Of course, he knew better than anyone as
a result of his pioneer work, *The Social Composition of Boards of
Education*, that school boards were composed of the privileged

and the powerful. Power has to be seized by the collective body of the teaching profession. But teachers, it seems, have little interest in power—this is one of the "certain ancient infirmities of the pedagogue,"[26] as Counts nicely put it. Counts recognized that if the schools are to gain and hold a central place in the education of the young, then the teachers must themselves gain and hold power.

This meant, at least initially, the collectivization of the teaching profession. To this end, Counts issued loud and persuasive calls. Not only that, but he also played a major and decisive role in the activities of the American Federation of Teachers, and flung himself into the middle of the communist controversy just prior to World War II. It was his leadership in ridding the American Federation of Teachers of community elements that saved the organization. Today, a majority of the nation's public school teachers belong to some bargaining unit, and while it is absurd to attribute this solely to Counts, he did play a major role as advocate and architect; thus one could not fairly maintain, as Theodore Sizer does, that his ideas "were never put into practice." The statistics belie that statement.

There is another respect in which Sizer is in error. Counts, with his solid background in sociology and anthropology, was perhaps the most eloquent spokesman of his time expounding the notion that to understand schools one must first understand the culture of which they are but a part. In theory at any rate, that idea is now a truism; it is indeed the backbone of comparative education—Counts has been called "the father of comparative education," and John Childs, writing to Counts on his retirement said, "Your work, along with that of Paul Monroe and Issac Kandel, helped to create this discipline."[27] The main body of his work, whether it dealt with America or Russia, demonstrates his deep interest in culture and schooling. In fact, his exposition of the relationship between the two is what gives his best work its timeless character. Times change, and society changes with them, but for the period from the late 1920s until the late 1950s, Counts pulled out the strands of American culture in a wonderfully prescient manner; he saw contemporary social forces with amazing clarity. But it is not simply the clarity with which he saw every detail that entitles him to hold a significant place in the development of educational thought; his place is assured essentially by the way he laid bare the relationship between schools and society. This has earned him a place in the stream of educational history.

Sizer may be correct in calling Counts "an educational visionary," but there is no evidence that Counts was unrealistic, as Sizer implies, in that vision. He saw some form of centralized control as necessary and inevitable in any modern, technological society. The question he asked repeatedly was whether that control would be used in the service of the privileged or of the common people. He advocated uncompromisingly that it should be in the service of the common people. The ledger is not yet closed, although considerable concern is now being expressed that corporate and powerful monied interests dominate government decisions. To call Counts "a visionary" simply because he would not accept the privileges of power as a given is to misunderstand his work. Doubtless that was the type of charge that bothered him, for he never missed the opportunity to point out that Utopia meant Nowhere, and the charge that he suggested we go Nowhere is bitter justice.

As mentioned earlier, Counts did not contribute much *directly* to the improvement of classroom practice. He believed that a teaching profession, one with power and true professional respect, would be in a position to make responsible educational decisions as well as responsible political ones. Therefore, there is nothing in his writings about education for life, the democratic classroom, and such matters. His is a cultural-political program, and inasmuch as teachers are nearer that goal, his career could be said to have been spectacularly successful.

But Counts is important in the history of American education (his influence on foreign education through his travels and lectures abroad, and through the impact of a large number of foreign graduate students who went through his hands cannot be negligible) for another, less talked about reason. This is aesthetic—a strange assessment, perhaps, of a person who had only a limited response to art and virtually none to music. His writing has a force and dignity, a simple, noble beauty that is unusual; it has none of the pomposity or ponderousness of much educational writing; it is completely devoid of jargon, yet it is not in any way precious or condescending; it has none of the obscurity of Dewey's (recognizing that Counts was not concerned, as Dewey was, with inventing a style), but it is neither shallow nor glib. As an educator, Counts does not have to play second fiddle in matters of style or syntax to any liberal artist.

Counts was a prolific writer. Much of his work was first delivered in speeches, which probably explains the immediacy of his style; it has the impact of a talk, and read aloud it stands up well. But when his work is pruned down to its essential ingredients, Counts's thought is not at all complex. His work can be divided into three parts, which do not exactly coincide with periods in his life. The first part consists of his early, empirical writings, done under the influence of Judd—such books as *The Selective Character of American Secondary Education*, *The Senior High School Curriculum*, *The Social Composition of Boards of Education*, and *School and Society in Chicago*. These are relatively unimportant today because the facts have altered, yet they demonstrate that not only was Counts well grounded in the use of empirical techniques, but also that his later generalizations were not simply spun out of the air, as has been charged. The other two parts of his work overlap and doubtless influence each other—his writings on Russia and those on American culture and education.

Counts was the champion of the rights of the common man. He himself was not so common, being, on his mother's side, a descendant of William Bradford, a leader of the Pilgrims, a signer of the *Mayflower Compact*, and a governor of the Plymouth Colony for thirty years.[28] This was a piece of autobiography that he rarely mentioned. He wanted to be identified with the people; special privilege, special treatment, the prerogatives of power were abhorrent to him. He never discussed his personal triumphs, and yet he was not a modest man in the sense of being self-effacing. It is touching that he inscribed for a British graduate student a copy of his book, *Education and the Foundations of Human Freedom*, thus: "Many, many thanks for the Magna Carta." The protestations legislated in the Magna Carta, outlined in the Declaration of Independence, found in the Constitution, and continued through statute and common law represent encouraging, if not consistent progress. Counts himself, that educator for a new age, played a small but significant part in that forward march of the common man.

2 American History and National Character

American Civilization—Our Heritage*

We possess a unique heritage. Although every country or nation
has its own peculiar history in which it may feel pride or shame,
we know that our history has followed a most unusual course.
This land that became America was settled more swiftly than any
other; and the great migrations thither were unlike the migrations
of other times. Moreover, as the decades passed into centuries
America came to represent in the eyes of her own people something distinctive in the long human struggle. She came to symbo-
lize certain ideas, certain values, and a certain way of life. Ever
since we embarked upon our great experiment in popular rule we
have been the source of both hope and fear among the nations of
the earth.

   We possess also a glorious heritage. Although many nations
have contributed mightily to human advance and many may
rightly sing of their achievements, the story of the rise of America
within a few generations to a position of unsurpassed power in the
world is one of the truly great epics of history. We have of course
had our dark moments and we have often been false to our finest
traditions. We have sometimes stoned our prophets, nourished our
prejudices, winked at injustice, practiced darkest bigotry, con-

*Education and the Promise of America (New York: Macmillan Co., 1945),
   pp. 28-51.

doned corruption in high places, and tolerated grievous exploitation of man by man. Yet as a people we do not celebrate these acts; on the contrary, we deplore them and cherish as the true expression of our genius the incomparable Declaration of Independence, the Federal Constitution and Bill of Rights, the Gettysburg Address, and our many struggles for liberty and justice. Ours has been a peculiarly happy and favored land, a land of opportunity and hope, a land of vast horizons and unlimited promise. Ours has also been a sheltered land. Never have we felt the iron heel of the conqueror; nor have we ever seen our republic swept from border to border by the fire of foreign armies.

To outline this heritage of ours in a few pages is obviously impossible. . . . The treatment here is frankly and deliberately selective in character. It is intended to be selective, within the limits of the possible, of the best in our history. It is an interpretation of our past designed to guide and shape the education of our children, to guide and shape our long future. Its veracity and worth must be left to the judgment of the American people. If they should reject it, no amount of scholarship could give it life. . . .

America was discovered and settled during one of the great revolutionary periods of history, at a time when mankind had struck its tents and was on the march. It was an age that witnessed the rebirth of science, the renewal of bold speculation concerning the nature of the universe, the release of creative powers of many kinds, and the general and rapid advance of knowledge, thought, and invention. Daring geographical explorations doubled the size of the known world, established the rotundity of the earth, opened up new sources of wealth, stimulated commerce and travel, revealed strange peoples and cultures, banished many ancient fears, and extended incredibly both the physical and spiritual horizons of the peoples of western Europe. Men experienced a sense of power and liberation that they had rarely, if ever, known before. The discovery and settlement of America were an expression of the spirit of this great age. And something of the audacity and hopefulness of that spirit has left an indelible mark on our civilization.

America was discovered and settled as the social system of the Middle Ages was disintegrating. New forms of economic production, new modes of warfare, and new agencies of popular enlightenment were undermining the material and spiritual foundations of the privileged orders and were bringing new social classes to power. At the same time the advance of knowledge and thought was weakening the authority of the church and turning the attention of men increasingly to the affairs of this world. America, moreover, was settled largely by people who in both their national and class origins were most fully and closely identified with these new forces. America was settled chiefly in the early days by Englishmen, and by poor, young, adventurous, dissenting, and even outcast Englishmen. This land was a haven of refuge also for men and women of many nations fleeing the oppressions and tyrannies of feudal institutions. It was a virgin seed-bed for the "dangerous thoughts" then agitating the mind of the Old World.

The spirit of the new Europe, struggling to be born, found the birth easier in America. Here were no vested rights and interests deeply and firmly rooted in law and custom. Here were few great landed estates that had been passed from father to son for generations and centuries. Here were few noble lords, of either church or state, who by armed retainers or by "motto and blazon" imposed their will upon the "rabble." Here were few prisons and dungeons and torture chambers for breaking the bodies and spirits of dissenters and rebels. Here, with rich and unoccupied land ever beckoning, men and women craving freedom could not be held in bondage. In remarkable measure, therefore, those who came to America were able to cast off the fetters of the past and make a fresh start in building a civilization. Although attempts were made to establish feudal ideas and institutions in America, these attempts were never really successful. Even to this day the term *feudal* carries a bad odor to the nostrils of our people. The fact that the present class structure of American capitalism has no support in feudal attitudes and outlooks surviving from a precapitalistic age is a source of great strength to our democracy.

As the modern age advanced, powerful movements for intellectual and political liberation, stemming in some measure from the ancient civilizations, swept through the more highly developed countries of western Europe. These movements, notably English rationalism and the French Enlightenment of the seventeenth and eighteenth centuries, were given a friendly reception by our people. A distinguished French historian has said that the ideas of the Enlightenment took deeper root in America than in France. Of these ideas, perhaps the most revolutionary was that of human progress and of the indefinite perfectability of man and his institutions. This idea found its natural home in America. The proposition that the future can be better than the past is an essential and even distinctive part of our heritage. Although it may foster an irrational optimism and may be narrowly interpreted, it is one of the great liberating ideas of history. Even our most conservative interests always claim to be marching under the banner of progress.

The American Revolution itself was a vigorous affirmation of the spirit of the modern age. Deriving its philosophy in part from the long tradition of political liberalism in England and the eighteenth century Enlightenment in France, from the ideas of Harrington and Locke, of Voltaire, Rousseau, and Condorcet, and in part from the life conditions of the New World, this revolution not only launched the greatest and most successful experiment in popular government in history but also reacted powerfully on the social ideas and institutions of the rest of the world. It helped to explode the age-old doctrine of the divinity of kings and aristocracies and encouraged people to revolt against their inherited and self-appointed masters. It caused tyrants to sit uneasily on their thrones and members of privileged orders to worry about their privileges. Our revolution served as a great sounding board to send certain ideas of the modern age around the world.

As the republic proceeded successfully on its course, it became a subject of discussion and controversy everywhere. Increasingly it aroused the fears of ruling classes, the hopes of the oppressed, and the interest of all. Generation after generation visitors from the Old World came to our shores in an endless stream—some to abuse, some to praise, some simply to learn. Millions came so that they and their children might live among us and join their blood and fortunes with ours forever. But that is another story. The thing to remember here is that the spirit of daring and adventure, the faith in man and his powers, and the promise of a better world which characterize the modern age constitute a priceless element in our heritage. To abandon these things, to become fearful of the future, to become engrossed in the defense of vested rights, would be to betray the genius of American history.

America has been populated over a period of more than three centuries by the greatest migration of history. During the one hundred years preceding the attack on Pearl Harbor approximately thirty-eight million men, women, and children crossed the great oceans and the borders north and south to make their homes in the

United States. In terms of numbers the migrations of all other times and places dwindle into relative insignificance. These immigrants and their descendants, from Jamestown down to the last boat entering an American port, have formed and are forming the American people. By their toil they have built our civilization.

This great migration, in comparison with earlier movements of peoples, has been unique. It was a migration not of clans or tribes or nations wandering away from the homeland, but rather of individuals and families forsaking by deliberate resolve their place of birth and moving by modern engines of locomotion to a strange and distant country. Though they doubtless endeavored to bring their possessions with them, they were forced to leave much behind, spiritual as well as material things. Also many possessions which they were able to transport across the oceans did not fit into the conditions of life in America. This fact compelled the development of a new civilization on the western shores of the Atlantic. It placed a premium on adaptability, inventiveness, and experimental temper. The migration, moreover, was a movement of many and diverse peoples—peoples diverse in race, language, and every aspect of culture. As a consequence America, throughout her history, has been the scene of a most extraordinary mingling and clashing of classes, religions, nationalities, and races. This fact also compelled our people to modify the institutions and ways of life which they had known in the lands from which they came.

At the time of the discovery by Europeans America was sparsely inhabited by a brave and vigorous native population living in a primitive stage of culture and probably derived originally from Asiatic sources. Though these people fought a losing battle with the newcomers from the Atlantic to the Pacific, they have left their mark upon us and have influenced our life and civilization. They have enriched our language, contributed much to our economy, altered our modes of warfare, and affected in some measure our moral and political ideas. Also they have contributed to the formation of the American stock.

The earlier migrations from the Old World were largely of Anglo-Saxon origin—people from England, Wales, and Scotland. Included among the first settlers also were many members of other races and nationalities, notably Negroes, Dutch, Swedes, French, Spaniards, Irish, and Germans. It was the British elements, however, that dominated the migrations down to the end of the colonial period and even into the early decades of the nineteenth century. These elements therefore have played a central role in the building of our civilization. They gave us our language, many of our political ideas and institutions, and innumerable cultural traits. Also, because of advantages associated largely with priority of arrival, they have tended to occupy in disproportionate numbers positions of privilege and responsibility in our life.

As the nineteenth century advanced and gave way to the twentieth, the source of the migration shifted again and again. Although immigrants continued to come from England, Wales, Scotland, northern Ireland, Africa, Holland, Sweden, France, Spain, and Germany, additional millions came from southern Ireland, Norway, Denmark, Belgium, Switzerland, Italy, Poland, the Balkans, Hungary, Russia, Finland, Portugal, Canada, Mexico, China, Japan, India, the Philippines, and other countries. These later migrations, moreover, not only brought new national and racial elements to America. They also brought new religious sects and faiths. To the original preponderantly Protestant population they added Jews, Roman Catholics and Greek Catholics, and even Mohammedans, Buddhists, and others. Today the people of America are no longer primarily Anglo-Saxon in their origins. It is estimated that the combined contribution of England, Wales, Scotland, and northern Ireland to the making of our population is well under one half, probably about forty per cent. The "typical American" is descended from many stocks.

These diverse peoples and their descendants, living and working together, are creating a new nation whose cultural and biological roots reach back to most of the countries of the earth and to most of the races of mankind. Some came early; some came late; the vast majority came because they wanted to come. Some came to escape oppression, some to avoid the jail or the rope, some to find adventure, some to make their fortunes, some to enjoy the liberties of the new land: they came from many motives. All, except those who were dragged into bondage or taken by force from their native lands, came to better their condition. All have helped to build America.

Each of these many peoples has made and will continue to make its contribution to the enrichment of our life and civilization. All of our present inhabitants, whatever their origin or time of arrival, whatever their race, color, or creed, are Americans and are entitled under our laws to all the rights, privileges, and responsibilities constituting the American birthright. No one of the many elements composing our nation, not even the Anglo-Saxon, can properly claim to be the "true Americans" or to be entitled to specially favored treatment. Whatever may be the practice, the fundamental law of our country makes no distinctions in citizenship. There are no citizens of second or third class. We are all simply citizens of the American republic.

This attempt to build a new nation out of elements from most of the races and peoples of the world is one of the greatest experiments of history. In the long run it may equal our experiment in popular government. It has of course increased our troubles and made more hazardous the operation of our institutions. Our different races, religions, and nationalities have often found it difficult to live and work together. Fears, jealousies, prejudices, and hatreds have marred their relationships from the beginning and have given the demagog or the bigot opportunity to put his perverted talents to work. They have warred among themselves and exploited one another. Yet the experiment has not worked out badly. Our civilization is richer, more varied and colorful than it would have been if our population had remained Anglo-Saxon. Moreover, in spite of the differences of race, creed, and nationality that still divide us, we are all united in our love of America. Few indeed there are among us, even among the most severely exploited, who would care to return to the lands from which they or their fathers and mothers came.

Today the great migration is over. Although immigrants will continue, perhaps for generations, to come to our shores in considerable numbers, the American people are here. The future of our country, therefore, the destiny of our civilization, is essentially in the keeping of ourselves and our children forever. The talents, actual and potential, of all the many elements of our population are the greatest resource of our nation. Here is the richest portion of our rich heritage.

From beginning to end the great migration was essentially a migration of common people—of people without pretensions of social rank or superiority. The records show that for the most part only the "middling and lower orders" of Europe came to America. During the century and a half following the first settlements a very large proportion of the immigrants were bond servants and Negro slaves. Also throughout our entire history many men, women, and children were persuaded under false pretenses to come to America by employers, steamship companies, and others seeking profit from the miseries of the Old World. Others, convicted of crime under the harsh laws of the age, were sent by force to penal colonies on this side of the Atlantic. The vast majority of the immigrants, however, came to America voluntarily and with some knowledge of the nature and conditions of the venture. In the course of time, consequently, there developed a glorious tradition about our country. America became a haven for the oppressed and the downtrodden, a land of opportunity for the poor, the underprivileged, and the dispossessed, a promise of redemption for the outcast, the criminal, and the damned of the earth.

Few indeed were the members of privileged classes who came to America. In the very nature of the case such people do not migrate, unless they are able to surmount the infirmities of their class, unless they are moved by love of adventure or devotion to ideals. Some of these certainly crossed the Atlantic and played a distinguished role in the development of the country. But as a general rule the privileged stay with their privileges. To leave the land where one is born and where one's ancestors lie buried requires powerful motivation. This is particularly true if the journey to the new country is long and hazardous, if life there is lacking in accustomed comforts, and if the language, institutions, and culture are strange. To the privileged classes of Europe the necessary motivation was commonly lacking. Moreover, it must be remembered that opportunity is always relative. What is opportunity for the poor may be servitude for the rich; what is opportunity for the man of courage may be hopeless risk for the coward; and what is opportunity for the idealist may be boredom for the lecher. To the privileged classes of the Old World, America was rarely a land of opportunity, at least not until these latter days when in the marriage market fortunes may be purchased with titles and pedigrees.

That America was settled by common people is in the record. It is equally in the record, however, that all of the common people, all of the oppressed and downtrodden, all of the poor and underprivileged of the Old World did not migrate to the New. Those who came must have been in some way exceptional. They must have rebelled against poverty and oppression; they must have had unusual faith in themselves; they must have had greater energy and daring than their brothers and sisters and neighbors whom they left behind. Nevertheless the fact remains that America has been in a very special sense a land of the common man.

The story of the rise of this common man to power in America is one of the most exciting in history. At the time of the early settlements he was often without property, without civic rights, without formal education, without social rank in the country of his birth. In many cases he was either just emerging or not far removed from serfdom. Here in America he gradually cast off the weight of centuries of oppression, rose to his feet, looked his "betters" in the eye, and became a free man. Given opportunities denied him in the older societies, he achieved confidence in himself, grew to a higher stature, and developed a new conception of his own worth, nature, and powers. It is even reported by aristocratic visitors from the other side of the Atlantic that he often became "downright impudent and disrespectful." Unquestionably he lost many of those qualities which the master finds so pleasing and charming in the servant.

Here in America this common man proceeded to storm the citadels of power in society. He gained possession of firearms, acquired skill in their use, abolished the military caste, and took into his own hands the elemental power to take life. He won the right to dispose of his own labor, acquired title to land and the tools of production, learned to manage his farm or shop in his own interest, and obtained a large measure of economic freedom and power. He conquered the right of suffrage, took over political processes and institutions, framed a bill of civil liberties, and created a "government of the people, by the people, and for the people." He established a free press, founded a system of public schools, gained access to knowledge and thought, and laid the intellectual foundations of human liberty. He separated church and state, proclaimed the principle of freedom of worship, and broke the hold of ecclesiastical authoritarianism over his mind. He even inserted in the immortal Declaration the affirmation that all men are created equal. Although these victories were never complete and although many battles won at one time have been lost at another, his total achievement has given hope to his brothers and sisters in all lands.

Here in America this common man led a further assault on the entire system of class and caste. He abolished the laws of primogeniture and entail. He nurtured the doctrine that the individual, regardless of ancestry or previous condition, should be judged only by his own industry, talents, and character and that he might aspire to the highest positions in the economic, political, and cultural life of the nation. Moreover, since he worked, and usually worked hard, for a living, he succeeded in giving to labor a dignity and a status not to be found in the societies of the Old World. Also, in very considerable measure, he pricked the ancient bubble of the innate superiority of the man of family and rank. The professed aristocrat, stripped of the artificial supports of tradition and caste, was often found to be quite an ordinary person. Here, therefore, the very idea of a social class, endowed with special rights and privileges, tended to become repulsive and un-American.

Perhaps the supreme achievement of this common man in America was the establishment of a system of constitutional government. As he struggled for independence from the mother country, he carried through a uniquely successful revolution. Building on the ideas of English political liberalism and the experience in self-government gained during the colonial period, he refused to follow the classical revolutionary pattern of the Old World with its cycle from dictatorship through armed revolt and military triumph back to dictatorship. He broke through this cycle and moved from victory on the battlefield to a novel and bold venture in statecraft. Led by a company of men of unsurpassed courage, inventiveness, and wisdom, he consolidated the gains of the revolution and fashioned a great charter of political rights and duties, processes and institutions designed to achieve liberty and justice, change and stability under a regime of law. In spite of heavy strains put upon it by the extraordinary growth and expansion of the nation, this charter has endured for more than a century and a half. Its authors hoped that it would make possible fundamental changes in economy and even government itself "without tumult, or the hazard of revolution." This is the central article of the American political faith.

The story of course is still unfinished. What this common man will do in the strange, complex, and dynamic industrial order which is sweeping the world, no one can say. That great trials and hazards throng the pathway to the future is evident. Yet this much is in the record: American civilization, whatever its merits or faults, is a monument to the powers resident in common people—in those millions of common people who in the course of more than three centuries came to this land and made it their home. Faith in America has always been faith in common people—in a common people capable of producing leaders of virtue and talent from its own ranks.

Every civilization must have a geographical base or home; and for any particular type of civilization some spots on the earth are far more choice than others. We possess in generous proportions one of those choice spots for the present epoch. In this respect we stand among the most favored of the nations. This land of ours is almost uniquely rich in those resources of climate, water, soil, forest, and minerals necessary to the development of a great, progressive, and enduring civilization in the industrial age.

The climate of America, the combined and varied action of heat, frost, moisture, and atmospheric pressure, is one of our most valuable resources. Its range and quality are exceptionally well suited to release the energy of human beings and to support the life of an extraordinary variety of valuable plants and animals. When an excellent climate forms a union with fertile soil, a land enjoys the richest gift that nature can bestow. These two resources are so ideally combined in America that there are few products of garden, field, orchard, or pasture, useful or pleasing to man, that cannot be grown somewhere in the country. We possess almost one-fourth of the arable land lying within the temperate zones of the earth. Originally our forests were unsurpassed. In their primeval state they were the finest to be found anywhere in the world and covered the colossal area of 850 million acres. In its mineral resources this land is perhaps the most favored region in all the world for the building of an industrial civilization. It has been said authoritatively that we possess "approximately 40 percent of the mineral reserves of the earth." While this estimate will probably have to be revised downward as we consume our inheritance and as more precise and comprehensive geological surveys are made on all the continents, and while certain important minor metals such as nickel, tin, manganese, platinum, and others, are found in insufficient quantities, the fact remains that we are among the most fortunate of peoples. Finally, our numerous streams and rivers, as they flow down to the sea, constitute a great source of energy to supplement the rich mineral reserves of coal and oil.

America is a beautiful land. As a forest draping slope and stream is more than timber for the mill, as a river winding among the hills is more than power for industry, as a mountain range pushing its snowy peaks into the clouds is more than ore for the smelting furnace, as an orchard in blossom in the springtime is more than fruit for the cannery in the autumn, or as a field of ripened wheat waving and billowing in the breeze is more than flour for the bakery, so this land with its "rocks and rills," its "woods and templed hills," is more than the source of our livelihood. It is our home, our dwelling place forever—the place where we are born and grow up, where we live and love, work and play, grow old and die. And it is a beautiful place as it comes from the hand of nature—beautiful in the grandeur and majesty of its great distances and proportions, in the contours and settings of its brooks and rivers, its ponds, lakes, and seas, in the lines and shades of its valleys, hills, and mountains, in the tints and colors of its forests, plains, and prairies, of its skies and horizons, in the rhythms of its calms and storms, of its days and seasons. "The valley of the Mississippi," wrote the great Frenchman, Alexis de Tocqueville, more than a century ago, "is, upon the whole, the most magnificent dwelling place prepared by God for man's abode."

This rich and beautiful land *was* a sheltered land. The expanse of the great oceans on either side, which guarded it from the wars and aggressions of the Old World, was for generations one of its most valuable resources. It gave to our people a sense of security and guaranteed to them the opportunity of relatively peaceful development. Safe behind her powerful natural ramparts, America was almost a world by herself. This is a resource, however, which we have no more.

This greatly favored land has left its impress on us and our civilization. It was the primary object of the great migrations. Like a powerful magnet it drew the peoples of the earth to its shores and then beckoned them onward toward the setting sun. It offered to the common man a chance to escape the harsh material deprivations and limitations of the Old World and to develop his own powers and institutions. It did much to arouse in him a hopeful, progressive, venturesome, and independent spirit. For almost three hundred years, as he moved westward with the advancing frontier, he was under the spell of a land that seemed almost boundless in extent and exhaustless in resources. But at last the geographical frontier was closed. Never again will we know the lure of the West. Never again will we know the security provided by the oceans.

Never again will we know a land so rich that we need not take thought of the morrow. That romantic epoch is gone beyond recovery.

As we look about this land today we are reminded of the parable of the prodigal son. Our heritage from nature is not what it was when the first settlers landed on the Atlantic coast. We have wasted much of our substance in careless, if not riotous, living. We have burned and slashed our forests; we have mined our rich soils of much of their fertility; we have skimmed the cream from our mineral reserves; we have marred the beauties of nature in a thousand ways. Yet America remains today a marvellously rich and beautiful land, a land capable of sustaining a great civilization for ages to come. But we need to realize that its riches are not exhaustless. We need to realize that this land, and probably this land alone, belongs to our children for century on century, that this land, and probably this land alone, must provide the geographical base of our civilization forever.

The People of America*

The long experience of the American people with popular government has tended to breed in them that elastic temperament which is essential to the successful operation of democratic institutions. They realize, at least in their more sober moments, that the introduction of sweeping changes into the social structure is not to be undertaken lightly, that even the best of minds cannot penetrate far into the future, and that simple solutions of complex social problems should be met with honest skepticism. Similarly do they know that the peaceful settlement of differences requires its own sacrifices, that the legitimate rights of minorities should be respected, that the possibility of error must ever be recognized, and that a spirit of compromise is preferable to blind loyalty to dogma or doctrine. While this temperament is doubtless less widespread and deeply rooted than might be desired, it is probably sufficiently strong to withstand shocks of considerable severity. Whether it will prove equal to the task of meeting the demands of

*The Prospects of American Democracy (New York: John Day Co., 1938), pp. 262-71, 283-86.

the coming struggle will depend, on the one hand, on the severity of the struggle and, on the other, on what is done in the meantime to propagate and vitalize the entire democratic tradition.

Closely linked with the democratic heritage is the experimental temper of the American people. Having been nurtured on the rationalism of John Locke, the French Encyclopaedists, and their successors, they have a deep faith in the powers of the human mind. Having broken with the past originally to cross the Atlantic and having broken with it again and again in the settlement and conquest of the continent, they tend to be impatient of the authority of tradition. Having passed with great rapidity through a succession of frontiers, having moved within a century from a simple agrarian order into a most advanced industrial society, having experienced in a few generations the transformation of most of the institutions of family and community, having changed their places of residence, modes of life, and social arrangements often and profoundly in the course of their relatively short history, they have acquired a mentality favorable to experiment and adventure. Although proposed changes in every field have commonly evoked the vocal and spirited opposition of a minority, the opposition as a rule has been overwhelmed. In a word the American people do not fear change as have most of the peoples who have lived on the earth.

More than that, they possess an outlook that welcomes change, that expects improvement from change, that regards change as an omen of good, that looks with hope to the future, that even tends uncritically to think of the new as better than the old. "Nobody," wrote Michael Chevalier of the American, "can conform so easily to new situations and circumstances; he is always ready to adopt new processes and implements, or to change his occupation."[1] This same observer quotes with approval a humorous passage from an unnamed American writer which reveals this characteristic confidence in the future: "We are born in haste; we finish our education on the run; we marry on the wing; we make a fortune at a stroke, and lose it in the same manner, to make and lose it again ten times over, in the twinkling of an eye. Our body is a locomotive, going at the rate of twenty five miles an hour; our soul, a high-pressure engine; our life is like a shooting star, and death overtakes us at last like a flash of lightning."[2] That such optimism reflected the unexampled opportunities for individual advancement, which at least for the time seem to have been checked, does not destroy it as a factor in the present.

Experience with change has bred in the American people a suspicion of prophecies of doom and a readiness to experiment. While this empirical and adventurous temper has thus far been particularly manifest in the realm of the material and mechanical aspects of the culture, yet the extreme popularity of Franklin D. Roosevelt suggests that it is already spreading to the sphere of economic and political arrangements. The worship of the constitution and the supreme court, for example, though carefully promoted, could scarcely long withstand their failure to function effectively. If the ordinary citizen exhibits an overweening loyalty to certain features of the social structure, it is probably because for a long period they have seemed to work unusually well. With the standards of living of the Old World ever in mind he has regarded himself among the favored of the gods. Let him become convinced that his institutions stand in the way of his interests and he will make comparatively short shrift of them. The fact that they are hallowed with antiquity will give to them a wholly illusory support.

The fact that the philosophy of instrumentalism developed in the United States is no accident. When in 1930 the University of Paris bestowed an honorary degree on Professor John Dewey, with whose name this philosophy is most closely identified, the Dean of the Faculty of Letters, in conferring the degree, characterized Dr. Dewey with true insight as "the most profound, most complete expression of American genius."[3] In the domain of practical affairs, where results can be checked, the average American is an instrumentalist by long experience. Paraphrasing Franklin, he does not inquire concerning an institution, *What is it?* but *What can it do?* Indeed he "instinctively" determines the nature of an institution by the manner in which it functions. He grasps quickly and eagerly the observation of Jesus of Nazareth that the Sabbath was made for man, and not man for the Sabbath. Also he tends to reject those neat systems of social logic, those "highfalutin" ideologies so congenial to the European mind which, while being great achievements of the intellect, tend to lose touch with the living reality, seek to force society into the artificial categories of a scheme of consistent propositions, and serve as false guides in grappling with the actual world in which men toil and struggle. As a consequence, not knowing the ultimate truth, he can escape that slavery to doctrine which has ever been the bane of civilized man and consigned millions to the torture chamber. He is ready to experiment, to judge by consequences, even to compromise. All of which is necessary to the operation of the democratic process.

That this predilection toward change, this practical and experimental temper, this scorn of theoretical knowledge has its dangers in the contemporary situation is obvious. Under the spell of the blind optimism nurtured by their history the American people may rush into strange experiments in economy and government without adequate intellectual preparation. Unfortified by general conceptions they may become the easy victims of some gifted demagogue. And yet it scarcely seems probable that they would ever behave more irrationally than that great people which for the past two centuries has dominated the field of systematic thought and philosophy—the German nation. If a country could be saved by its theorists, the Second Reich certainly would not have succumbed to the mad proposals of Hitler. Perhaps the experimental temper of the American people will prove dangerous only if it is not informed.

The economic individualism of the frontier and the farm which the great majority of the American people practiced for generations was far less rugged and ruthless than many champions of the virtues of calculated selfishness would have the present generation believe. It was tempered in the family group by a spirit of cooperation and mutual helpfulness: it was tempered in the sphere of community relationships by a spirit of "good neighbourship" and simple human kindliness. Isolated and self-sufficient individuals, living by the principle of "each for himself, and the devil take the hindmost," could never have conquered and settled the North American continent. The curbing of egoistic impulses and the pooling of resources and energies were demanded on innumerable occasions. In an economy without money, without extensive division of labor, without a dependent class of slaves, serfs, or wage earners, voluntary exchange of services, paradoxically, was "compulsory." According to Tocqueville, cooperation was fostered by that very "equality of conditions" which produced the individualism of the many. This equality, "whilst it makes men feel their independence," he wrote, "shows them their own weakness: they are free, but exposed to a thousand accidents; and experience soon teaches them that, although they do not habitually require the assistance of others, a time almost always comes when they cannot do without it."[4]

In the presence of danger or disaster these "individualists" often enforced severe discipline, despising as cowards or loafers all who refused to share the burden of defending the general welfare. For two and a half centuries the settlers along the frontier carried on an intermittent but pitiless struggle with the Indian—one of the most courageous and warlike races ever to face the white man. Frontiersmen of both sexes arranged their dwellings and planned their common life in order to meet the threat of attack from the savages. For the same reason, as they migrated toward the Pacific, whether by trail or waterway, whether through the forests, across the plains, or over the mountains, they advanced in bands and companies more or less well organized and disciplined. Also they combined to protect themselves against the depredations of horse-thieves and bandits, against the ravages of floods, droughts, and pests. Their recognition of the community interest went so far as to deny the rights of private property to fish, game, bee trees, wild nuts and fruit, and within limits even the produce of orchard and garden.

They were always ready to come to the aid of the individual or family in distress, whether friend or stranger. "When an American asks for the cooperation of his fellowcitizens," observes Tocqueville, "it is seldom refused; and I have often seen it afforded spontaneously, and with great goodwill. If an accident happens on the highway, everybody hastens to help the sufferer; if some great and sudden calamity befalls a family, the purses of a thousand strangers are at once willingly opened, and small but numerous donations pour in to relieve their distress."[5] And this assistance was usually proffered without a thought of charity or feeling of self-righteousness, it being well understood that no one is immune to the visits of misfortune.

But perhaps the most striking and significant form of cooperation was called forth by those varied tasks and undertakings which tended to exceed the powers of the individual family or which lent themselves peculiarly to group performance. Indeed, these early individualists seem to have found much of their recreation and social life in occupational "festivals" which still survive here and there in vestigial form. Great numbers of activities were made the occasion for community gatherings and cooperative effort. John

Bradbury thus describes and interprets this feature of American rural life as he saw it:

It is necessary to remark, that in the early part of the settlement of a country like this, a great number of things occur necessary to be done, which require the united strength of numbers to effect. In those parts, money cannot purchase for the new settler the required aid; but that kind and generous feeling which men have for each other, who are not rendered callous by the possession of wealth, or the dread of poverty, comes to his relief: his neighbours, even unsolicited, appoint a day when as a *frolic*, they shall, for instance, build him a house. On the morning of the appointed day they assemble, and divide themselves into parties, to each of which is assigned its respective duty; one party cuts down the trees, another lops and cuts them to proper lengths, a third is furnished with horses and oxen, and drags them to the spot designed for the site of the house: another party is employed in making *shingles* to cover the roof, and at night all the materials are ready upon the spot; and on the night of the next day, he and his family sleep in their new habitation. No remuneration is expected, nor would it be received. It is considered the performance of a duty, and only lays him under the obligation to discharge the debt by doing the same to subsequent settlers. But this combination of labour in numbers, for the benefit of one individual, is not confined to the new comer only, it occurs frequently in the course of a year amongst the *old settlers*, with whom it is a continued bond of amity and social intercourse, and in no part of the world is *good neighbourship* found in greater perfection than in the western territory, or in America generally.[6]

Certain interesting details are added in an account by John Woods, an Englishman who from the vantage point of an English settlement in Illinois in 1820-21 made a competent study of American life and customs on the frontier. After describing a "Husking Frolic," he observed that while the English settlers harvested their corn without recourse to group action, "the Americans seldom do any thing without having" a frolic:

Thus, they have husking, reaping, rolling frolics, &c. &c. Among the females, they have picking, sewing, and quilting frolics. Reaping frolics, are parties to reap the whole growth of wheat, &c. in one day. Rolling frolics, are clearing wood-land, when many trees are cut down, and into lengths, to roll them up together, so as to burn them, and to pile up the brushwood and roots on the trees. I think this one is useful, as one man or his family can do but little in moving a large quantity of heavy timber. Picking cotton, sewing, and quilting frolics, are meetings to pick cotton from the seeds, make clothes, or quilt quilts; in the latter, the American women pride themselves. Whiskey is here too in request, and they generally conclude with a dance.[7]

James B. Ireland, "looking backward through one-hundred years" of life in Kentucky, tells how these group undertakings looked to a participant and explains something of their philosophy:

It was slow, laborious work clearing the land of the heavy timber. In the fall of the year people would raise houses and barns and in the spring every man would have a log rolling. I would lose a week or two at a time in the busiest part of the year helping my neighbors roll logs. Every one had to be neighborly in self defense. If you did not help others, others would not help you. This log rolling was no fun. Men would go early, work hard and late. At dinner time they would gather around the Spring, quench their thirst and wash their blackened hands. The bottle and sugar would be set out. All would take a toddy and sit down to a good dinner which had been cooked in pots and skillets around the fire place or outside under a shed and which the women took great pride in serving. We would be treated to hog jowl, fried eggs, turnip greens, corn bread, fried ham, hot biscuits, butter and butter milk, winding up with half moon fried pies and maple molasses. In order to make one dinner answer two purposes the women would frequently invite their friends the same day to a quilting or wool picking.[8]

Charles A. Beard, in a recent communication to the *New York Times* in which he takes issue with certain statements made by James Truslow Adams in an article printed in the paper the week before, gives vigorous expression to the cooperative and neighborly aspects of the old frontier and farming life. Mr. Adams had said that "on each frontier the same fundamentals were driven home. A man had to depend upon himself. He made his clearing, built his house, and sowed his crops or hunted game. With no police or courts, he was a law unto himself." In responding Mr. Beard writes in part as follows:

The frontier was crude in many ways, no doubt. The English language was badly treated, in a fashion somewhat Elizabethan. But the frontier was far removed from the harsh, materialistic picture which Mr. Adams and his colleagues are fond of giving us.

Now I come down to the individualism business. Neither the man nor the family stood alone, save perhaps in isolated cases. No individual man could build himself a log cabin or make a clearing without help. If he had no near neighbors, his wife took the other end of the cross-cut saw. But generally he had neighbors. They "swapped" work. It was a common thing when a couple was married for the neighbors to gather, cut trees, and build a cabin for them.

The spirit of the frontier as I knew the pioneers was not the spirit of individualism that characterizes the war for trade, jobs and profit in the cities.

Pioneers were individuals, of course, and had a strong sense of individual responsibility—perhaps stronger than some of the great bankers in charge of fiduciary trusts in 1928. But pioneers were not striving to get trade or jobs away from the neighboring pioneers. Their profit was the spirit of neighborly helpfulness—in work, in times of adversity, in hours of celebration.[9]

Some may argue that this tradition of "good neighbourship" is wholly a thing of the past, that it is dead, that it has left no imprint on the character of the American people. And they may be correct. Perhaps it has been destroyed by the pecuniary standards of capitalism, by the impersonal relationships of the great industrial society, by the deep divisions of interest that shake the contemporary economy. But all of this is mere speculation. Whether the tradition still lives can be ascertained only by appealing to it. If it has in fact disappeared with the conditions from which it sprang, then no appeal can evoke a response. There is evidence, however, that it still possesses some vitality. The predilection of the American people to join organizations, their well-authenticated generosity in the presence of suffering, and their readiness to respond to leadership devoted to the general welfare suggest that it only awaits the direction appropriate to the new age. At any rate those who would make democracy work in the present epoch of close interdependence cannot afford to ignore or repudiate this possible resource from the past. Perhaps the central social task of the age may be defined as the application of the old principle of "good neighbourship" to the great neighborhood of today.

.   .   .   .

Although certain of the nations of Europe doubtless equal or surpass the American people in the realm of intellectual and artistic achievement of the highest order, it seems probable that the cultural level of the masses in the United States is unusually high. For more than a hundred years the dominant aim of the educational agencies of the country has been the dissemination of knowledge among the people, even though standards of excellence had to be sacrificed in the process. While this practice has called forth much criticism from abroad and even from the intellectual classes at home and while it has not realized the fond hopes of its advocates and progenitors; while the opportunities have been extended quite unevenly to the various regions and population elements; and while an honest and realistic program of civic and political educa-

tion has never been attempted on a large scale, yet the work of the
formal educational agencies combined with the experience of living under institutions which have been relatively free has given the
rank and file of the citizens a large measure of political sense and
understanding. The fact that they may not be as far advanced in
their command of systematic social knowledge and theory as certain European peoples is to be attributed primarily to the ease of
life in America and the absence of that impulsion to think, which
must come in large part from the environment. Given the need,
and apparently the need is now being given, the American people
can be counted upon to render a very satisfactory account of
themselves in the sphere of political discussion, thought, and action. The example set by their fathers in the first seventy-five years
of the history of the Republic would seem to justify this conclusion. Let them once become clearly aware that there is something
wrong in their democracy and they may be expected to strike their
political tents.

Such a generalization is suggested by the recent behavior of the
American people. Mr. Gallup, on the basis of his unique experience, concludes that the "public mind is remarkably alive to the
issues of the day," that the "typical American is highly articulate
on questions of public policy," and that "by and large, the majority of voters seem to have an acute sense of values—a ready ability
to distinguish reality from sham." He also states that the "institute
has found no evidence" of that "fickleness" which the critics of
democracy in all ages have attributed to the people.[10]

Perhaps the most striking vindication of the political sense and
independence of the American people was shown in the presidential campaign of 1936, when reactionary elements resorted to
every device known to demagogy to discredit Franklin D. Roosevelt and his administration in the eyes of the public. In the prose-
cution of their attack they possessed, besides almost unlimited
funds, the voluntary services of the representatives and agencies of
entrenched wealth. According to an analysis of the record of the
daily press in the fifteen largest cities of the nation made by the
New Republic, "approximately 71 percent of the total circulation
of the fifteen cities . . . was hostile to Roosevelt."[11] And three-
fifths of the circulation favoring the President were in New York
City. With almost no newspaper support in the country, with old
Democratic papers going over to Mr. Landon, and with the short

end of the radio program, Mr. Roosevelt found himself charged daily with the intention of destroying the American form of government and society. It was said that he was following the lead of both Stalin and Hitler, that he proposed to introduce into the United States both fascism and communism, that he intended to regiment both labor and business, that he had nefarious designs on both large and small enterprise, that he desired to destroy both property and liberty. It was a new and manifold edition of Theodore Dwight framed in the hopes and fears, loves and hates of the fourth decade of the twentieth century. In addition employers, according to an old tradition, endeavored to frighten their employees with the threat of insecurity should Roosevelt be reelected.

And what was the response of the American people, lacking a press and without adequate organization, to this unprecedented barrage of accusation, recrimination, misrepresentation and downright falsification? They went to the polls and voted overwhelmingly for the president, placing but two small states in the Landon column—states that have not yet fully emerged from the preindustrial epoch of American history. Regardless of the merits of Mr. Roosevelt and his program, a subject about which there is much room for debate, the election of 1936 registered one of the greatest victories for democracy ever achieved in the United States. The American people exhibited wholly unexpected powers to resist political propaganda—one of the best possible measures of the political sense and civic competence of a people.

3   Education and Social Forces

Education and Choice*

When we begin to seek a firm base for an education suited to our age, we encounter at once a most obvious and, at the same time, a most fundamental truth: education is always a function of some particular civilization at some particular time in history. It can never be a purely autonomous process, independent of time and place and conducted according to its own laws. It is as much an integral part of a civilization as is an economic or political system. The very way in which education is conceived, whether its purpose is to free or enslave the mind, is a feature of the civilization which it serves. The great differences in educational philosophies and practices from society to society are due primarily to differences in civilization.

A civilization, however, does not generate an education imper-sonally as a tree generates fruit. Nor is education derived automat-ically through a process of analysis and assembling of data. Always at the point where an educational program comes into being defi-nite choices are made among many possibilities. And these choices are made, not by the gods or the laws of nature, but by men and women—men and women moved by all of those considerations that move them in other realms of conduct—by their knowledge and understanding, their hopes and fears, their purposes and loyal-ties, their views of the world and human destiny. Presumably a

*Education and the Promise of America (New York: Macmillan Co., 1945), pp. 23-27.

given society at any given time therefore might formulate and adopt any one of a number of educational conceptions or programs, each of which would obviously be an expression of its civilization. But each would also be stamped by the special qualities of the men and women who framed it. These men and women in turn would be authentic, but not exclusively authentic, products of their civilization.

The formulation of an educational conception or program is thus a creative act, or rather a long series of complex creative acts. It is a threefold process embracing analysis, selection, and synthesis. It always involves choice among possibilities, and even decision as to what is possible. It likewise involves the affirming of values and the framing of both individual and social purposes. Inevitably education conveys to the young responses to the most profound questions of life—questions of truth and falsehood, of beauty and ugliness, of good and evil. These affirmations may be expressed in what an education fails to do as well as in what it does, in what it rejects as well as in what it adopts. The total education of a people, the education that goes on from the day of birth, both in and outside the school, shapes with overwhelming power the character and destiny of that people. In its organized phases it is deliberately designed to make of both the individual and society something which otherwise they would not become. The launching of an educational undertaking therefore is a very serious business. It is one of the most vital and responsible forms of statesmanship.

The age now unfolding . . . is the most critical age of our history. We face great troubles at home, powerful revolutions and counter-revolutions abroad, unprecedented responsibilities in the world, a future of almost limitless possibilities for good and evil. In the decades ahead our democracy may be transformed into some form of totalitarian despotims or it may march from triumph to triumph and fulfill gloriously and nobly its historic promise.

The age calls for a truly great education—an education commensurate in conception and in practice with the hazards and the opportunities of these times, an education for freedom and humanity equal in power to the education of any existing or possible totalitarian system. Such an education, however, cannot be derived from the concept of efficiency, from the interests of children, or even from a study of the "great books" of the Western World. It can come only from a bold confronting of the nature, the conditions, the values, and the potentialities of our civilization. An education can rise no higher than the conception of civilization that pervades it, provides its substance, and gives it purpose and direction.

Our first responsibility therefore is to formulate on the foundation of fact a conception of American civilization in its historical and world setting. We must ask ourselves in all soberness what we are "up to" on this continent. Only when we have answered this question, and answered it magnificently and powerfully, will we be in position to draw the broad outlines of a great education for our people in the coming years. If we can find no answer, or if we find a mean and feeble answer, our education, however efficiently it may be conducted, will at best be mediocre and uninspired. . . .

The Public School*

Every educational policy, however casually it may have been constructed, rests upon and reflects some analysis and interpretation of the condition and prospects of the society involved. If education were merely a form of abstract contemplation, unrelated to the world of men and things, the social situation might be disregarded altogether. This, however, is clearly not the case. At bottom and particularly in a highly complex and dynamic social order, education, in discharging its function of inducting the child into the life of the group, stands at the focal point in the process of cultural evolution—at the point of contact between the older and the younger generation where values are selected and rejected. In the case of organized education presumably all of this is done rationally and deliberately and in the light of some large conception of welfare. For the educator to seek justification for evasion, inaction, and postponement in a profession of ignorance is to issue a proclamation of incompetence. Such a course is no more seemly for him than it is for the statesman.

The obligation of the educator to base his policies on as profound an analysis of social life as he is capable of making can best be expounded by first examining the relation of education to social action. About this question there seems to be a good deal of confusion.

*The Social Foundations of Education (New York: Charles Scribner's Sons, 1934), pp. 532-63.

The American people have a sublime faith in the school. They have traditionally viewed organized education as the one unfailing remedy for every ill to which man is subject. And when faced with any trouble or difficulty they have commonly set their minds at rest sooner or later by an appeal to the school. Today, as social institutions crumble and society is shaken by deep convulsions that threaten its very existence, many persons are proclaiming that education provides the only true road to safety. They are even saying that it should be brought into the service of building a new social order.

In an earlier generation this faith took the form of a trust in simple literacy. It was confidently assumed that if all men could read, everything would be well. The mass of voters, according to the argument, being able to follow the course of events and being keenly aware of their own interests, would keep the ship of state on an even keel and hold it firmly on its course toward the distant goals of democracy. How insecure were the foundations of this faith is revealed by the confusion which now pervades the public mind in every country whose citizens have been initiated into the mysteries of reading. Apparently the printed page has become an instrument of deception as well as of enlightenment. Powerful interests employ it to mold the public mind and to gain support for their policies. Literacy made possible the age of propaganda.

More recently the faith in education has taken a new form. The assumption now seems to be widely held that the entire process of cultural evolution should begin *de novo* with each generation, that the child should be completely freed from the bias of the past, and that the program of instruction should contain no great decisions with respect to the values and ideals of living. Such decisions should presumably be left to the next generation in the firm belief that, if boys and girls could only once escape the rule of parents and elders, they would proceed unerringly and with enthusiasm to the correction of all the mistakes of their ancestors and to the building of a world founded on truth and beauty and justice. Thus is education converted into a substitute for positive thought and action on the part of the present adult generation.

There is every reason for believing that this faith also will prove to be unfounded. It represents in fact an unwitting confession of bewilderment on the part of its proponents. It is a refuge of ignorance—an escape from reality—a shirking of responsibility. It is, moreover, quite beyond the limits of attainment and is certain to bring disillusionment. Inevitably education *is* a form of action—enlightened or befuddled, depending on the social insight of its author. An educational program that is a product of bewilderment will itself beget bewilderment. The more difficult problems of society will not be resolved by passing on to children facts whose implications are beyond the comprehension or the courage of adults. In the selection of facts to be transmitted, moreover, large decisions are made.

If education is to grapple with a given social situation, it must incorporate a social philosophy adequate to that situation—a social philosophy that has substance as well as form—a social philosophy that represents great historic choices. Education, emptied of all social content and conceived solely as method, points nowhere and can arrive nowhere. It is a disembodied spirit. When education is thus generically conceived, it is a pure abstraction. Moreover, it is not education. A practicable educational program or theory cannot be generic: it must be specific: it must be suited to a particular time and place in history. If adults assume that, after becoming mentally confused, they may deposit their confusion on the doorstep of education and then retire to peaceful slumbers, they are only deceiving themselves. They are placing their trust in a modern form of sorcery.

Society possesses no such easy road to the future. Education will be called upon to play its part. But it will be an education that is carefully designed, both as method and as content, for the present day and generation. It will be an education that recognizes the impossibility of moving in all directions at once, that chooses deliberately and intelligently one fork of the road rather than another, and that does not hesitate, when occasion warrants, to make fundamental decisions regarding national destiny. Ordinarily, moreover, these grand choices will be made for children by adults. To think otherwise is to chase rainbows. Any concrete school program will contribute to the struggle for survival that is ever going on among institutions, ideas, and values; it cannot remain neutral in any final and complete sense. Partiality is the very essence of education, as it is of life itself. The difference between education and life is that in the former partiality is presumably reasoned and enlightened.

That education involves positive action and decision with respect to many matters is entirely obvious. Those in charge of an educational institution must make innumerable choices before the institution can begin to function. And each choice involves rejection as well as selection. Thus choice has to be made with respect to physical surroundings. Here far-reaching decisions regarding aesthetic values are necessarily involved. The school building will represent, not all styles of architecture, but some particular style. Likewise the wall decorations will reflect some standard of taste. Even the door to a classroom will be given a definite location. If these questions about physical surroundings are viewed as unimportant, then this in itself is an expression of a very fundamental choice. Much the same line of analysis may be applied to the selection of teachers, of subjects or fields of study, of textbooks and equipment, of methods of instruction. Of peculiar significance is the way in which the life of the school is organized—the relations of pupils to pupils, of pupils to teachers, of teachers to teachers, of teachers to administrators and supervisors, and of all to the public. Any organization will express some theory of government and will tend to generate certain ideas and values. As William T. Harris observed many years ago, the child "simply gets used to established order and expects it and obeys it as a habit. He will maintain it as a sort of instinct in after life, whether he has ever learned the theory of it or not."[1]

Then every school must make some decision concerning the motives to which to appeal in stimulating and guiding the process of learning. At no point can the school assume complete neutrality and at the same time become a concrete, functioning reality. It is concerned with a growing organism; and growth must have direction. The determination of this direction is by far the most crucial of all educational problems. Whether this responsibility is to be discharged by parents, teachers, politicians, statesmen, or various powerful minority groups is not the question at issue here. But whatever the agent, the responsibility must be discharged.

A fact never to be forgotten is that education, taken in its entirety, is by no means an exclusively intellectual matter. It is not merely, or perhaps even primarily, a process of acquiring facts and becoming familiar with ideas. The major object of education since the beginning of time has been the induction of the immature individual into the life of the group. This involves not only the development of intellectual powers, but also the formation of character, the acquisition of habits, attitudes, and dispositions suited to a given set of living conditions, a given level of culture, and a given body of ideals and aspirations. Contemporary American society would seem to require quite as much emphasis on moral education as any primitive tribe.

The foregoing argument, however, is not intended to convey the impression that education, since it involves a large measure of imposition, requires a severe regimentation of the mind, a rigorous teaching of a body of doctrine as fixed and final. However adequately such a conception of education may have served certain of the relatively static societies of the past, it would be extremely dangerous in the highly dynamic social order of today. A distinctly critical factor must play an important role in any educational program designed for the modern world. An education that does not strive to promote the fullest and most thorough understanding of society and social institutions, of which childhood and youth are capable, is not worthy of the name. The child should not only be permitted, he should be encouraged, to question all things. But this does not mean that a particular educational program may not be dominated by certain great social ideals. In fact no social ideal merits support today that does not make generous provision for the free play of intelligence.

The role of critical intelligence in the educative process, however, must bear some relation to the maturing of the individual. Immaturity in the human race is a very real and remarkable fact. When the members of the species enter the world, they are in an extremely helpless and undeveloped condition. The process of maturing, moreover, goes forward with exceeding slowness. During the first months of life the infant is entirely dependent on his elders. At this time his every act must be carefully watched lest he suffer serious injury, form wrong habits, or expose himself to unfavorable environmental conditions. Doubtless much of the debate over the amount of freedom to be extended to the learner arises out of failure to delimit the age under consideration. While in a university graduate school of science the educative process may be reduced to its bare intellectual elements and the student practically freed from the restraints of tutelage, the work of the kindergarten, the primary school, or even the secondary school has to be conceived and organized in quite different terms. This of course does not mean that the interests of children should not be utilized at every level of instruction. But it does mean that the extent of guidance provided by the older and more expert members of a group must vary inversely as the degree of maturity.

If education is to be regarded, like statesmanship, as a form of action, involving the making of positive decisions with respect to national destiny, any body of citizens charged with the responsibility of shaping educational policy must relate their recommendations to the great trends of the age. In the case of the American people, the most profound truth here is that they are passing from an individualistic to a collectivist economy. The meaning of this change for education will be considered from the standpoint of its bearing on purpose, curriculum, and teaching personnel. And under curriculum emphasis will be placed on the social sciences. . . .

The most fundamental conclusion for education implied in the data presented in this volume is that the present age requires a radical revision of the controlling purpose of the American public school. This is due to the fact that, since the founding of the institution, interdependence has replaced individualism in the sphere of economy. Here is the fundamental reality that cannot be escaped. Here is the great guiding conception of any educational program capable of serving contemporary society. Educators might wish that it were otherwise, but their wishes would be of no avail. From this verdict of history there is no appeal. To resurrect the loosely organized economy of the world that created "the little red schoolhouse" is impossible. That economy has been overwhelmed by the onward sweep of technology. The school of the twentieth century must function in an economy that in its basic structure is becoming thoroughly socialized.

Beyond this point, however, . . . the facts would seem to leave some room, indeed enormous room, for choice. Presumably the collective economy, involving, as it does, the close integration and coordination of the productive energies of the entire population, might be organized primarily in the interests of some ruling caste or privileged minority, possibly composed of those holding title to property. To the masses of the people would go a fixed quantity of goods and services, a kind of balanced ration for the human animal, perhaps scientifically determined so as to sustain him at the optimum level of working efficiency and to inoculate him against the harboring of revolutionary ideas. Given the premises of such a society, to do more would be a form of economic waste. The remainder of the social income, increasing with the advance of science and technology, would accrue to the members of the aristocracy and be employed to protect them in the enjoyment of their privileges and to enrich their lives in every way that human ingenuity could contrive—to support a police and military force of sufficient strength to intimidate the populace and to quell occasional uprisings, to convert the more beautiful and pleasant portions of the country into extensive parks and playgrounds for their exclusive use, to maintain vast and numerous estates and menages as forms of display, to transfer to the domain of personal service the surplus labor occasioned by the increased use of automatic machinery, to provide opportunities for luxurious travel over the continent and the world in search of comfort or some new sensation, and generally to maintain a life of leisure and extravagance that would far surpass anything of its kind in history. The fact that membership in this caste might shift gradually from generation to generation through the operation of some sifting process sanctified by the name of individualism, freedom, or democracy would not greatly alter the situation. Indeed such an arrangement would merely increase the stability of the social order and serve as an insurance against popular revolt. It is of course entirely patent that the American people, without being aware of it, have been drifting toward a collectivist society of this kind for several generations.

The purpose of popular education in such a society is easily discernible. The major function of the school would be to inculcate into the minds of the rising generation the idea that the existing institutions, including practices with respect to the distribution of wealth and income, power, privilege and opportunity, were expressions of the immutable laws of human nature. The school might also serve to select out of each generation the more energetic and gifted, those most likely to become actively discontented, and lift them into positions of privilege, if not directly into the ranks of aristocracy. The children of the ruling caste, on the other hand, would be sent to special schools designed to instill into them a feeling of superiority and to teach them the language, the manners, the sports, and the outlook upon the world suited to their class. They would also be made to feel that their privileges rested upon the sanction of nature or divinity.

The social situation, however, undoubtedly contains a second possibility of broad dimensions which is far more in harmony with the deepest loyalties and aspirations of the American people. Conceivably, a closely integrated economy might be managed in the interests of the great masses of the population. Under such an arrangement no class or group would be regarded as a means for the elevation of another, no aristocracy of either birth or property would be allowed, no great concentration of wealth or income in private hands would be permitted, no grinding poverty or degrading slums, placing their indelible stamp on the generations, would be tolerated. On the contrary, the moral equality of all men, as proclaimed in the Declaration of Independence, would be recognized as a controlling ideal and would be accepted as a guiding principle in the reconstruction of social life and institutions. The productive energies of the nation would be devoted first to laying the foundations of material security for all. Thereafter they would be dedicated to raising the cultural level and enriching the lives of the people, to making the entire country a pleasant and beautiful place in which to live. The natural endowment and the resources of technology would be administered in the name of society as a whole. According to evidence advanced elsewhere in this volume, an economy, not only of security, but of abundance lies within the realm of the possible. The American people merely lack the will, the knowledge, and the discipline necessary to achieve it.

That educational leaders, at least if they are speaking for the public school, must make the second choice is fairly obvious. Whatever may be their legal position, they represent the masses of the American people and are therefore under obligation to protect the interests of those masses. The second choice, moreover, as already pointed out, carries on and fulfills the great tradition of democracy. If this ideal of human worth is to survive, it must be transferred to the foundations of a collective economy. Public education in the United States therefore will not only work within the limits of the emerging reality; it will also assume that the evolving order will make paramount the welfare of the great rank and file of the working men and women of the nation.

If the argument up to this point is sound, then the purpose of public education in the present epoch of American history is clear. It is to prepare the younger generation for labor and sacrifice in building a democratic civilization and culture on the foundations

of a collective economy. This means in very considerable measure
the abandonment of ideals that have dominated the school for generations. In spite of many protestations to the contrary education
is still regarded primarily as a road to special privilege and personal
aggrandizement. The motive that drives parents to send their children to high school and college and that drives boys and girls
through the routine of the curriculum is the allurement of preferred occupational and social status. As a consequence, under the
inherited system of arrangements, knowledge and competence acquired in schools maintained at public expense are often turned to
the purpose of the exploitation of the handicapped. At a time
when the economic struggle was primarily between man and nature, the result was perhaps defensible; today, when the struggle
involves increasingly the relationship of man and man, the result
is intolerable.

The aim of public education now should be, not to elevate A
above B or to life gifted individuals out of the class into which
they were born and to raise them into favored positions where
they may exploit their less fortunate fellows, but rather to abolish
all artificial social distinctions and to organize the energies of the
nation for improving the condition of all. In industrial society men
do not and cannot live alone. The school should be permeated, not
with the competitive, but with the cooperative, spirit. It should
strive to serve society as a whole, to promote the most inclusive
interests. This does not mean that it would refuse to give knowledge and competence to the individual, but rather that with knowledge and competence it would give a strong sense of social obligation. It would then be concerned primarily not with the promotion of individual success, but with the fullest utilization of the
human resources of the country for the advancement of the general welfare. The result, moreover, would not be to deny the individual the joys attending successful accomplishment. On the contrary, his successes would be as genuine as ever and might even be
far more profound and satisfying than they are when recorded in
purely personal terms.

Perhaps the most serious charge directed against the traditional
education is that it holds out no great ideal capable of enlisting the
loyalties and disciplining the energies of childhood and youth.
This of course is the logical result of the attempt to build a school
program on the foundations of economic individualism, which in

the very nature of the case can scarcely be regarded as a social ideal. For individualism is a divisive rather than a unifying force, and tends to reduce organized society to the role of policeman. In the earlier years of the republic the ethical defects inherent in the economy were softened somewhat by the solidarity of the family, the neighborliness of the small community, the passion for political democracy, and the idealism of Christianity. The efforts to correct these defects today are often both pitiful and tragic. On the one hand, children are nourished on moral platitudes that bear little relationship to the current social reality. And on the other, they are taught a brand of patriotism that is identified with the glorification of war and of willingness to bear arms. Such a narrow conception of patriotism is the perfectly natural fruit of a society which achieves unity of purpose only when it organizes to repel invasion by a foreign foe or to engage in military conquest. In an integrated society definitely committed to the democratic ideal, men would find glory and honor in the struggle with nature and the war on poverty, pestilence, ignorance, injustice, and ugliness. An education intelligently harnessed to such a purpose would merit the fullest support of the entire population.

The reference to war suggests that the ideal here proposed cannot be identified with a narrow nationalism. Technology has bound the nations together only less tightly than it has united the inhabitants of a single country. The economic foundations are being laid for the integration of the world and the curbing of the forces of competition in the international no less than in the domestic field. Indeed, in view of the devastation wrought by war conducted with modern weapons, the achievement of the former might seem to be even more urgent than the achievement of the latter. Yet, it should not be forgotten that the two forms of competition are not to be clearly distinguished and that the one may be transmuted into the other. Thus the ideal of interdependence must not be confined within the limites of a narrow patriotism. The great purpose of the public school therefore should be to prepare the coming generation to participate actively and courageously in building a democratic industrial society that will cooperate with other nations in the exchange of goods, in the cultivation of the arts, in the advancement of knowledge and thought, and in maintaining the peace of the world. A less catholic purpose would be certain, sooner or later, to lead the country to disaster.

The primary object of the curriculum, which should be thought of as embracing the entire life of the school, as well as the so-called subjects of study, should be the fulfillment of the great purpose just outlined. Indeed that purpose should permeate every activity of the school and give unity to the entire program. The more significant implications of this position for the curriculum as a whole and particularly for the social sciences will be briefly indicated. But since the present volume is directed primarily toward the teaching of the latter, the reference to the total program will be highly abbreviated.

The reconstruction of the curriculum in the light of the democratic ideal operating in a world marked by economic interdependence would not call for the addition of new subjects. Indeed, to superficial observation, perhaps no important changes would be discernible. The same disciplines would be taught; the same activities would be organized. Children would learn to read and write and figure; they would work and play together. But the spirit, the approach, the orientation would be different. Pupils and teachers might be doing the same things as before, but the motivation would follow unwonted channels. The appeal to the egoistic and possessive tendencies would be strictly subordinated; the emphasis everywhere would be placed on the social and cooperative and creative impulses. From the earliest years the whole life of the school would be organized so as to bring out and strengthen these qualities. No individual would be rewarded merely for overcoming or surpassing another.

This does not mean that high achievement would be frowned upon or that a single standard of mediocrity would be imposed upon all. Indeed, quite the contrary would be the case. In a closely integrated society the fullest development of the varied gifts and abilities resident in the population is demanded by the common welfare. Such would, in fact, be one of the major objects of organized education. To fail here would involve, not merely a dwarfing of the individual concerned, but the impoverishment of the group. To overlook personal talent in any field of social usefulness or cultural worth would not only involve a form of injustice, but would also be tantamount to wasting a valuable natural resource. Such a thing might happen, but it would be the result either of folly or of inefficiency. The springs of achievement, however, would be different. All would be united in the common task of raising the material and cultural level of the total population.

Also the emphasis on social utility, which might be expected in an interdependent society, does not mean necessarily that education would be narrowly practical. The stress would depend no doubt in considerable measure on the richness of the natural resources, the level of technology, and the pressure of population on the means of subsistence. In a land marked by severe struggle for the bare necessities of life, the emphasis might indeed be restricted to "bread and butter" considerations. But in a land like America, where material security and abundance are easily possible, the opposite should be expected. With the removal of competition in the display and conspicuous consumption of goods and services, energies would presumably be released for cultural and spiritual development. Economic concerns might at last be forced into a definitely subordinate role in society. And this would of course be reflected in the educational program.

The several divisions of subject matter composing the curriculum would all be given a social meaning. This may be illustrated by reference to geography, science, and art. Geography would be taught and studied, not merely as a body of information useful and interesting to the individual, but as the physical basis for the building of a finer civilization and culture. The natural resources of the nation would actually be regarded as possessions of the nation—as the source of a richer and more abundant common life, rather than as fields for the operation of profit-seeking enterprise and the accumulation of great private fortunes. In similar manner, science and technology would be looked upon neither as a leisure-time activity of a special class nor as an instrument for personal aggrandizement, but rather as the spear-point of man's age-long struggle with nature. And art would be taught primarily, not as a vehicle of individual expression, as important as that is, but as a means of enriching and beautifying the common life. Instead of spending itself in museums and galleries and the private homes of the rich, it would bring beauty of line and form and color to factories, cities, highways, parks, great public buildings, the objects of ordinary use, and the dwellings of the people. All of the subjects of study would be integrated by the mighty and challenging conception of the building of a great industrial civilization conceived in terms of the widest interests of the masses.

Finally, a word should be said about provision for specialized training. A society based on a collective economy would of course require proficiency in the entire range of occupations, except those which are definitely predatory or parasitic in character, such as advertising, speculation, and racketeering. Vocational training, however, would always be given a social purpose. Care would be taken lest the specialist regard his training as a species of private property which he is entitled to exploit at the expense of the general population. Also the program of occupational preparation would be approached and organized from the standpoint of the needs of society rather than in terms of the ambitions of particular institutions, departments, or persons. In other words, an effort would be made to coordinate the training facilities of the country and, in the case of each calling, to meet the requirements of the economy. Such of course is the implication of any comprehensive scheme for economic planning.

Much more could be written regarding the reorganization of the curriculum as a whole which is demanded by the emergence of the new economy. The object of the present treatise, however, does not permit the further elaboration of this topic. Attention will therefore be directed to the problem of the teaching of the social sciences.

The point should be made at the outset that there is nothing in the social sciences themselves that compel their inclusion in any educational program. In fact throughout the major part of the history of the school these subjects occupied a distinctly minor, if not a negligible, position in the curriculum. Whether or not and in what measure they are to be included is a question of social and educational philosophy, informed of course by the findings of the social scientist. From the standpoint of the school, however interesting and significant they may be to the investigator or the scholar, they are but means to some desirable end. They must take their chances with Sanskrit, astronomy, and automobile mechanics. Yet, since education itself is a social process and therefore a proper object of study for the social scientist, the relation between education and social science is always extremely intimate.

In the light of the analysis of American life presented [earlier]— an analysis derived from data furnished by the social sciences— American society is seen to be in transition from a loosely organized to a closely integrated economy. Also that analysis reveals the presence in American history of a great ideal which presumably will continue to give direction to the evolution of American institutions. The selection and the organization of materials in the teaching of the social sciences therefore will be determined by the needs of a society that is moving from individualism into some form of collectivism conceived and administered in terms of the interests of the masses of the people. It is within this framework that the social sciences will have to function in the schools.

This is not to say that the social sciences are to be converted into an instrument of propaganda, that history is to be falsified, or facts suppressed. To pursue such a course would be to court disaster. Any sound program of instruction must rest upon and utilize the findings of science. This is not a debatable question. And yet it is equally obvious that the social sciences themselves possess no inner logic that can be relied upon to furnish positive and adequate guidance in the selection and organization of materials. They merely place at the disposal of the educator a practically inexhaustible body of data and generalizations, bodies of knowledge and systems of thought, regarding the history and functioning of human institutions. As to whether American children should study the life of Australian aborigines, the marriage customs of the ancient Romans, or the rise of parliamentary government among the Anglo-Saxon peoples, they are completely silent. Until some purpose is agreed upon or some set of values injected into the situation, choice among available materials is irrational and without meaning.

The controlling purpose to be employed here has already been outlined. The social science instruction in American schools, according to the argument, is to be organized within the frame of reference provided by the ideal of a democratic collectivism. From the standpoint of such a frame of reference, it is argued here that the social science curriculum should include the following points of emphasis: the history of the life and fortunes of the masses of the people, the evolution of peaceful arts and culture, the development of the ideal of democracy, the rise of industrial civilization and collective economy, the conflicts and contradictions in contemporary society, the critical appraisal of present-day life in terms of the democratic ideal, and the thorough examination of all current proposals, programs, and philosophies designed to meet the needs of the age.

In the first place, the social sciences should be called upon to prepare for the coming generation a fairly accurate and comprehensive account of the lives and fortunes of ordinary men and women throughout the ages and in diverse societies, but focused upon the course of events in the western world and culminating in the modern age in America. An effort would be made to piece together the record of how the masses of the people have lived, worked, played, loved, worshiped, thought, and died; how they have governed and been governed; how they have toiled and struggled to raise themselves above the brute. Certainly, in a society "dedicated to the proposition that all men are created equal" such an emphasis would seem to be far more rational than the traditional stress on the doings of aristocracies, princes, kings, and emperors. And it should be observed, incidentally, that social science itself offers no clue as to whether the one or the other emphasis should be adopted.

In the second place, the social sciences should be asked to tell the story, as fully as time permits, of the evolution of the peaceful arts and culture. While this principle is perhaps subsumed under the first category, since wars have commonly been the concern of ruling classes, it is of so great importance, from the standpoint of the ideal chosen, that it merits separate consideration. The conclusion should not be drawn, however, that war ought to be ignored altogether. This institution has played too tragic and central a role in human history to be deleted from the record. The distinction between wars of liberation and wars of conquest would be recognized. Also in general the treatment of military conflict would be altered. The object of the account would not be to prepare the mind of the coming generation for the profession of the soldier, as in the past, but rather to give understanding of war as a social phenomenon that has brought much misery and suffering into the world. Warriors and military leaders would be placed in a minor role, and attention would be concentrated on the great creative spirits of the past—the inventors, the explorers, the organizers, the statesmen, the teachers, the scholars, the scientists, the artists, the philosophers, the prophets of mankind. The fact would be stressed throughout that human culture is not the product of any single nation, but the common achievement of the efforts of many races and peoples working and striving through the ages.

In the third place, the social sciences should trace in broad outline the development of the ideal of democracy. And here there should be no disposition to accept a narrow definition of the ideal or to confine attention to its evolution on the North American continent. Rather should it be identified with the emergence of the conception of the worth and dignity of the common man. As such it would lead to certain of the great religions of the past and to various revolutionary and humanitarian movements in the modern world—to the overthrow of chattel slavery, to the liberation of the serf, to innumerable popular revolts against privileged classes, to countless struggles for human liberty, to the emancipation of woman from many ancient disabilities, to the growth of organized labor, to the abandonment of various forms of cruel and inhuman punishment, to the spread of ideas of tolerance and cooperation, and to the rising demand for the abolition of war as an instrument of national policy. Since the program of instruction is being devised for American children, a realistic and unvarnished history of democracy in the United States should be presented. This is peculiarly necessary because of the practical disappearance of the conditions that nourished the ideal for several generations.

In the fourth place, the social sciences should recount in considerable detail the growth of industrial civilization and the emergence of an integrated economy. The drawing of a sharp contrast between the life of today and that of the generation which founded the union would be peculiarly illuminating. The development of science and technology and the growth of man's power over nature would be brought into the center of the picture. Also the repercussions of these new forces in the various departments of life would be observed and studied—in family relations, in economy, in communication, in health control, in education, in recreation, in art, in religion, in government, and in morals, thought, and philosophy. The account might well culminate in a consideration of the passing of *laissez-faire*, the reunion of economics and politics, the rise of social planning, and the movement toward world integration and organization.

In the fifth place, the social sciences should be required to describe the conflicts and contradictions so numerous in contemporary society—prosperity and depression, poverty and riches, privation and extravagance, starvation in the midst of plenty, organized destruction of wealth, preventable illness and unemployed physicians, great inventions converted into instruments for the debasement of culture, scientists engaged in the discovery of "secrets," costly art museums in ugly and congested cities, an avowed democracy ruled by a plutocracy, corruption of government by respectable businessmen, the widespread subordination of human to property rights, the Church of the carpenter of Nazareth accepting gratuities from entrenched wealth, whole nations rushing to war in the name of peace, the general subordination of the ends to the means of life, and the many other conflicts and contradictions listed in the present volume. The younger generation is entitled to an honest and unprejudiced account of these strange phenomena.

In the sixth place, the social sciences should provide youth with the materials for a critical appraisal of present-day life in terms of the democratic ideal. To transmit this ideal to school children, without at the same time providing the opportunity for applying it rigorously to the criticism of existing institutional arrangements and practices, would be the height of intellectual dishonesty. Yet this is precisely what has been done in the past. As a consequence, when boys and girls, after leaving school or before, learn how the world is actually run, they tend to rate their teachers as either knaves or fools. If the school is to function at all in the betterment of the social order, it must expose pitilessly and clearly the shortcomings in contemporary society. It should never convey the impression that the democratic ideal has been fulfilled in the United States. To do so would be to draw a heavy veil over the eyes of youth.

In the seventh place, the social sciences should be required to introduce the coming generation to all the more pertinent proposals, programs, and philosophies that have been called forth by the needs of the age and that show any signs of strength. Among these should be included such social theories as capitalism, syndicalism, anarchism, socialism, guild socialism, distributism, communism, and fascism. Also wherever any of these theories are being given trial in the world today, opportunity for the careful study and fair appraisal of the results should be systematically provided. No idea should be kept from the minds of youth on the grounds that it is dangerous. Each proposal, however, should be critically examined in the light of American history and the ideal of democracy. Not to permit this free flow of thought will be far more inimical in the long run to the best interests of society than any undesirable consequences that might arise from allowing young persons to become acquainted with a new idea in the classroom and under the tuition of a competent scholar. The present situation demands informed intelligence of the very highest order distributed widely throughout the population. The days of complacency with respect to inherited institutions and conceptions are over. If the people of the United States cannot think their way through the great difficulties that lie ahead, then must they be prepared for the twilight and then the night of democracy.

Questions regarding ways of organizing and methods of presenting the materials of instruction in the social sciences are essentially far less important than questions of content. Regardless of form the fundamental ideas embodied in any program will be grasped by the better minds of the coming generation and thus be incorporated sooner or later into the main body of social thought. And the great need in American society today is for a radical increase in the breadth and the depth of the ideas in general circulation. The first task therefore is to advance the quality of the content of social science teaching in the public schools. If only books dealing competently and thoughtfully with the social situation in its historical and world setting could be made widely accessible to the more able members of the younger generation, the gain in raising the intellectual level of the population would be infinitely superior to that derived from the mere refinement of method, however thoroughly done. It is sheer folly to assume that the world will be much improved by doing mediocre or irrelevant things excellently.

The organization of the content to be taught, however, is a matter that cannot be ignored. If instruction is to proceed, there must be some organization; and there are doubtless better patterns to follow. That any effective plan for the presentation of materials must take into account the experience, the powers, the interests of the learner is entirely obvious. A more fruitful guiding principle, however, may be found in the process whereby the child grows to maturity in social understanding and competence. Beginning with the cradle he gradually pushes back the boundaries of his world along the two dimensions of space and time and in so doing widens his knowledge and deepens his powers of thought and action. Through manipulation, exploration, travel, reading, social intercourse, and converse with his peers and elders, he moves out from the immediate and the present into the ever-widening realm of geography and history.

Social science instruction in the schools should build upon, facilitate, and direct this process. It should take the child in the first year of the elementary school and lead him systematically and steadily out of family, neighborhood, and community into the state, the nation and the world, always following naturally those lines of trade and communication which bind the near to the remote and create a general condition of interdependence. In similar fashion, pursuing the genetic method, it would move from the present into the past and back again and give understanding of customs, institutions, ideas, interests, and conflicts. Also as the child matures and advances in intellectual grasp, the emphasis would shift from the surface to the depths and from data to thought. The point merits great emphasis, moreover, that the isolation of the school should be reduced to the narrowest possible proportions and that "classroom instruction" should be closely bound into the life and labor and aspirations of society. Thus from the kindergarten through the secondary school and on into the college and university there would be on unbroken and integrated social science program which would carry a single process to ever wider and more intense expression. Permeating and vitalizing this program from bottom to top would be the great purpose of organizing the energies and resources of the nation in improving, enriching, and refining the common life of the people.

Such a conception of the task calls first of all for the preparation of an extensive body of printed materials to be used in the home, the school, and the library. Primary reference is made here, not to textbooks, necessary as they may be, but to a children's literature which will illuminate the modern world and express the spirit of the industrial age. Much of the children's literature bequeathed from the past, while worthy of preservation because of its artistic excellence, contributes nothing to social understanding. Also a considerable proportion of the reading matter employed in the lower grades to train children in the habits of literacy possesses neither literary merit nor useful content. The great need is for rich materials written with charm and simplicity and designed to give to children authentic information regarding the human past and the world of today—materials which tell in story form of the evolution of basic social institutions, the achievements of the race, the diversity of peoples and cultures, the rise of American civilization, and the manifold characteristics, tasks, problems and potentialities of industrial society. On such a foundation the more systematic study of the social sciences would be organized.

The present volume, as well as the other reports of the Commission, assumes from first to last that the public school may be expected to make a genuine and positive contribution to the solution of the numerous social problems confronting the American people. It assumes that education, as a function of organized society, can exercise some measure of social leadership, or at least that it can make somewhat easier the difficult road to the future. Whether or not this faith is well founded will depend in the last analysis on the teacher, and particularly on the social science teacher. If the person presiding over the classroom is meanly gifted, if he is inadequately or inappropriately prepared for his post, if he lacks a clear and sufficient conception of his responsibility, and if he is surrounded by unsuitable working conditions, there is no hope. Commissions may come and commissions may go; they may leave voluminous reports behind them; but if the teacher remains substantially unchanged, the schools will be as ineffective as before, even though numerous alterations of school procedures may be introduced. New testing devices, new methods of instruction, new courses of study, unless they impart new knowledge, power, and spirit to the teacher, are but the gyrations of a treadmill. Attention will therefore be directed to the crucial questions involved in the selection, training, and working conditions of teachers.

The question of the selection of teachers is fundamental. Yet it depends in no small measure on the conditions of work which society provides for those who are to have charge of its children. . . . Unless young men and women of intelligence, spirit, capacity for leadership, and devotion to the popular welfare are drawn into the schools, very little can be expected of public education. Without these qualities teachers may indeed continue to be obedient to their superiors, meticulous with respect to small matters, mindful of the wishes of the most powerful and respectable forces in the community. They may even succeed in holding their jobs, unless a depression cuts severely into the social income. But as a profession they will not rise to the level of educational statesmanship; they will not influence the course of history, except perhaps to do what they can to equip children for a world that is gone and thus add to the difficulties of social adjustment. Leadership in society requires courage and competence.

If it may be assumed that gifted persons in reasonable numbers will be drawn to teaching, the next problem is that of training. Although in a technical sense teachers are far better prepared today than ever before, the ordinary training program is woefully inadequate to the task outlined above. To be sure, the country is well supplied with normal schools, teachers' colleges, departments of education, and universities. Yet nowhere, with very few exceptions, are the issues being squarely and fully met.

The major difficulty seems to lie in partial or erroneous conceptions of the nature of the educative process. In the special training schools the emphasis is too generally placed on the mastery of the methods and techniques of teaching and on what is called the science of education. The inevitable result of pursuing such a program of preparation is a narrowing of the intellectual interests of the student and an absorption in the mechanics rather than the substance of teaching. The concept of the science of education seems to rest on the assumption that an objective study of the processes of learning and of administering education will result in the discovery of certain laws of procedure that are largely independent of and superior to culture. If this assumption is sound, then a systematic study of American history, institutions, and ideals is quite unnecessary. The difficulty is that the essence of any actual educational program is intimately related to the evolution of a particular culture.

If one turns to the various special departments of the university for an enlightened form of teacher training, the situation is found to be equally unsatisfactory. If the teachers' college is lost in the science of education and the cult of pedagogics, the university department, whether it be language, science, or history, is lost quite as completely in its pursuit of highly specialized knowledge. The latter very commonly even prides itself on its devotion to a species of scholarship that has no interest in the practical affairs of men. Then when it accepts the responsibility of training teachers, it assumes that this peculiar academic mentality should be introduced into the secondary and even lower schools. So the prospective teacher is too often compelled to choose between two types of preparation, neither of which represents an adequate conception of the task of teaching. The one would equip him for action divorced from deep understanding; the other would prepare him for understanding matters that can have little or no relation to any desirable or probable form of action.

The need is for a new type of training institution—an institution which would embody the best features of the two types already described. A college for the preparation of teachers should first of all be a center of liberal learning—a center through which would run the main currents of modern thought. It should be a place for the study of American culture in its historic and world connections, but for a type of study that would not be purely academic in character. In the halls of any institution devoted to teacher training, the past and the future should meet; the most profound questions of national policy should be debated and understood. And this should be done, not as an intellectual exercise, but for the purpose of shaping educational programs. Out of such an institution should come persons genuinely qualified to provide American communities with a vigorous, enlightened, and public-spirited type of leadership, ready and competent to challenge the power of selfish interests and to champion the cause of the masses of the people. The attention devoted to purely technical preparation would assume extremely modest proportions. On public education, as on statescraft, the findings and thought of the social sciences should be brought to a focus.

If teachers were given this type of training, they would in all probability immediately demand proper conditions of work. The question, however, is of such importance that it should not be passed over altogether.

That teachers should have adequate compensation, reasonably secure tenure, and a high degree of freedom from annoyance at the hands of educational laymen is axiomatic. Moreover, being products of American institutions for the most part, their loyalty to the deeper ideals of the nation cannot be questioned. Since they are the servants of society as a whole, they may generally be expected to be at least as disinterested in the promotion of the common good as any other body of citizens. Without security and freedom professional competence is impossible. In order to get these conditions, teachers should organize and place their case forcefully, intelligently, and persuasively before the public. Because of the peculiar difficulties of their subject matter . . . the teachers of social science are under special obligation to make this appeal effective.

Of equal importance is the matter of administrative organization. Under the influence of the mechanistic and atomistic psychology which swept through education during the past generation, a theory of school administration took root that might well prove disastrous to the public schools. According to this theory, it is the duty of the teacher to take orders from the head of the department, of the head of the department to take orders from the principal, and so on from level to level of the supervisory hierarchy. As a result, in many school systems teaching has become largely a matter of following instructions received from some official not immediately responsible for the work with children. The tendency was no doubt accelerated by the ideal of efficiency derived from big business and by the spread of the so-called objective tests. A school system thus took on the aspect of a vast and intricate mechanism designed to pass on to the younger generation certain reading habits, number combinations, and facts about geography, history, and civics. Needless to say, this entire procedure represents a travesty on education, primarily because it tends to destroy the personality and initiative of the teacher. The first object of any policy of school administration should be the growth of the teacher in courage, power, and refinement. Under such a policy, if it should become widespread in the nation, able young men and women would be attracted to the profession in ever-increasing numbers. Education then might grapple with the most profound problems of national policy.

This consideration of the responsibilities and opportunities of the school under the conditions of industrial civilization may well be concluded with a reference to the relation of school and society. Here a word of caution will be uttered regarding the powers of organized education.

Although the school is the focal point of the educative process and the only form of education under the conscious and reasoned direction of society, its power for influencing social change is strictly limited. Various studies undertaken by the Commission, as well as others, make this fact altogether clear. Industrial society is marked by various powerful and competing groups and interests, each of which seeks to impose its will upon the school. The task of steering the course of public education among these conflicting forces requires the highest qualities of leadership.

The primary aim here, however, is to direct attention, not to the play of social forces upon the school, but rather to the number and strength of the nonscholastic educational agencies. Thus, the family, in spite of its loss of functions during the past century, remains by far the mightiest single formative influence in the life of the individual. There are also the time-honored agencies of church and community association which, though weakened, continue to mold the minds of the young. Then there are those relatively new instrumentalities that have either appeared or waxed powerful since the rise of industrial civilization—the press, the library, the cinema, the radio, and various other forms of communication. While the school has grown with great rapidity during the past two generations and may now be regarded as a major social institution, it is clearly but one among many educational agencies. Consequently, if it is to become a positive factor of any great strength in American society, its programs and policies will have to be intelligently conceived and efficiently executed. Teachers in particular are inclined to exaggerate its influence, partly because of the widespread tendency in America to identify education with the work of the school. It is well therefore that they be asked from time to time to view this institution in proper perspective.

Moreover, as organized and administered in American society, the school is greatly weakened by the artificiality of its activities. In a word, the school tends to be definitely separated from life. For generations educators have lamented this fact and have argued most cogently for a more intimate relationship between organized education and the community. But their laments and arguments have seemingly fallen on deaf ears. The school continues in its tradition of isolation; and teachers as a rule have relatively little contact with the real world. Francis W. Parker once said that "the best-taught school in a densely populated city can never equal in educative value the life upon a good farm, intelligently managed." Although he was perhaps speaking under the romantic spell of the farming tradition in America, his statement contains a large element of truth.

The fault, however, would seem not to rest primarily with the schools or the teachers. The fact cannot be stressed too strongly that in capitalistic society, where large areas of life are reserved to the operation of business enterprise, a sharp line divides public from private interest. It is this line that educators have been unable to pass. As a consequence, the school is forced into an artificial world and organized education is pushed out upon the periphery of existence. In order to meet this situation, which is a product of very recent development, educational philosophers have evolved the doctrine that children have interests quite unlike those of adults and should therefore organize a society of their own. According to this doctrine, the school should become a second society in which boys and girls would be permitted to live a full and rich life. The idea has had many and able advocates. Yet it would seem to be a totally inadequate conception. A genuine society is composed of neither children nor adults, but of persons of all ages living together in close interdependence. It is in such a setting that life goes on. And until such a setting is provided for the school, organized education will be lacking in genuineness.

Any completely satisfactory solution of the problem of education therefore would seem to involve fairly radical social reconstruction. The fact is that for the most part contemporary society is not organized primarily for the education of its children or for the achievement of any other humane purpose. Such matters are largely subordinated to the processes of wealth production and accumulation. Even the recreational, cultural, and aesthetic interests of the population are exploited for material gain. Nothing is permitted to "injure business." This is axiomatic in the inherited social order. Yet it clearly means an unnatural and irrational transposition of values.

This condition can be corrected . . . only by the clear and frank recognition of the collectivist character of industrial economy. The productive energies of the country will then be directed squarely toward the laying of the material foundations of a great civilization and society will be organized to foster the cultural and spiritual development of the masses of the people. In the achievement of the second purpose all the educational resources of the community will be coordinated and utilized to the fullest. The press, the cinema, and the radio will no longer be devoted to profit making. Travel will doubtless take the place of textbooks in many instances. Even industry will again become an educational enterprise. It may also be discovered that many of the burdens placed upon the school during the past century can best be borne by other agencies. The scope of operations of the school may consequently be greatly reduced and children may again be inducted into the life of the group through actual participation in the activities of society. But in the meantime the school, whatever its strength or weakness, is under obligation to devote its energies to the task of bringing such a society into being.

4 Technology and Industrialism

The End of the Agrarian Age*

When in the year 2000 the historian writes his account of the period through which we are now passing, how, I often wonder, will he appraise the various educational tendencies of our generation. He will no doubt have something to say about the extraordinary extension of educational opportunity, the structural reorganization of the educational system, the almost universal concern with curriculum making, the differentiation of the program of higher education, the so-called progressive education movement, the development of teachers' colleges, the tremendous growth in educational expenditure, the widespread interest in the scientific study of education, and numerous minor changes in the structure and procedure of our schools and colleges. From his vantage point in time he will be able to assess in terms of their fruits that vast medley of currents and movements which now disturb the educational consciousness. Some he will find good, others bad, and perhaps many sterile. Certain tendencies which we regard today as full of promise he may leave out of the record entirely, while others which now appear insignificant he may bring into the center of the picture.

But let me hasten to reassure my hearers that I have no intention . . . of donning the garb of the historian three-quarters of a century hence and of thus seeking for my own pronouncements a wholly spurious authority. To do so would be to assume the role

*Secondary Education and Industrialism (Cambridge, Mass.: Harvard University Press, 1929), pp. 1-12.

of a prophet, and history tells us that prophecy is a dangerous business. My hope rather is that we may detach ourselves from the present situation and view the problem of secondary education from a distance, and consequently in perspective. Let us assume therefore that when our historian speaks he is merely ourselves striving to view the contemporary social and educational landscape from afar.

In at least one respect the historian of the future will, I think, find our attack upon the problem of education gravely deficient. He will see us extremely busy with many things, some of which are important; but he will be amazed at the absence of any vigorous and concerted effort to discover the educational implications of the new industrial civilization which is rapidly overwhelming and transforming the traditional social order. He will see, as we apparently do not, that we have been literally precipitated into a new world: a world which with a ruthless and relentless energy is destroying inherited values, creeds, and faiths; a world which is demanding new social arrangements, a new legal code, a new ethics, a new aesthetics, a new religion, and even a thorough-going revision of our ideas regarding the nature of man. He will see us in this strange fantastic industrial society repeating formulae handed down from an agrarian age when we should be searching with tireless effort for formulae suited to the world as it is; he will see us preoccupied with educational techniques and the minutiae of school keeping when we should be wrestling with the basic problems of life; he will see us greatly agitated over the construction of an algebra test or a marking scale, when we should be endeavoring to make the school function in the building of a new civilization.

Until well towards the close of the last century, or until little more than a generation ago, we were essentially a rural people but recently emerged from a pioneering economy. Except for the older regions east of the Alleghenies and widely scattered trading centers standing at the junction of railroads and water courses, the nation was composed of small communities based upon agriculture and linked together by bad roads and horsepower. The small, semiindependent, partially isolated, and largely self-sufficient agricultural village with its rural hinterland constituted the social unit of this agrarian society.

The social fabric, however, was no more simple than the lives which we led. We lived close to the soil and in intimate touch with

nature. Most of us earned our daily bread by the sweat of the brow
and we knew the joys and the sorrows of exhausting physical toil.
With bodies bowed beneath the burdens of clearing forests, breaking virgin land, building homes, and bearing children, both men
and women grew old in middle age. Life for us was a grim struggle
with the elements, material comforts were despised, physical prow-
ess and courage were idealized, and the refinements of culture
were unknown. Our recreations were crude, our religious beliefs
primitive, our intellectual horizon narrow, our educational needs
limited. And yet an abundance of fertile land, the absence of
hereditary social classes, and the participation of practically all
members of society in manual labor made men socially and politi-
cally free—as they have seldom been free in human history. It was
in a society of this type that the American system of public education took form.

Today, except for survivals in remote and inaccessible areas and
the memories stamped by experience upon the minds of the generation now passing off the stage, this old agrarian order is a thing
of history. Through invention piled upon invention a marvelously
intricate and comprehensive network of railroads, boulevards, telephones, mail routes, newspapers, automobiles, radios, and airplanes
has demolished mountain ranges, contracted plain and prairie, and
destroyed the isolation that had nurtured individual independence
and social differences. Steam, electricity, and petroleum, harnessed
by mechanical contrivance, have given to men the strength of gods
and made possible a mobility of commodities, persons, and
thoughts which distinguishes our society radically from all other
societies issuing from the womb of time. And hand in hand with
these advances in the realms of transportation and communication
have gone revolutionary changes in the economic order: the universal introduction of power-driven machinery, the formation of
gigantic industrial combinations, the minute differentiation of labor, the improvement of agricultural tools and processes, the specialization of whole regions in production, the mastery over the
forces of nature of which men in the past could only dream, and
the development of an all-pervading system of finance and credit
upon whose delicate balance the functioning of our entire economic structure and the material prosperity of all of our people depend.

More far-reaching perhaps in their effects upon human life than the material changes themselves are the new social relationships which they have generated. The intimate personal connections which held the small rural community together have been super-seded by relationships predominantly mechanical and impersonal in character. Apparently the associations necessary for the func-tioning of the more complex society are so numerous that in the interests of mental economy they must assume a mechanical qual-ity. The human mind simply cannot apply the spirit of the neigh-borhood to all of the transactions necessary to life under industri-alism. Consequently, following lines set by social function, we have been compelled to divide the social world into numerous categor-ies and to develop fixed mechanical responses towards both per-sons and events. In no other way could we manage intellectually the huge, complex, swirling sea of forces which has engulfed us.

A vast area of our relationships has been reduced to a certain form of order by the application of the pecuniary principle. A visi-tor from our old agrarian civilization would view with incredulous eyes our practice of equating all things in terms of a monetary unit. In order to provide for the easy exchange of goods and ser-vices made necessary by the extreme specialization characteristic of industrial society we have set a price on everything from ditch-digging to healing the sick and from beefsteak to works of art. The simulation of personal interest in the welfare of his intended vic-tim has become a part of the salesman's technique; and there are those who would say that even what remains of friendship and vir-tue may be bought and sold in the open market. Obviously the problems of human living set by this strange child of science and invention are many and difficult. Men have suddenly been thrust into a world altogether unlike that in which the race was cradled and in which human culture has evolved in the past.

This is not the place to evaluate industrial civilization. It has both its protagonists and detractors in abundance. Some contend that it has ushered in the golden age of material plenty, removed the curse of crushing toil, extended to all classes the god-like gift of leisure, made man the master of his fate, freed the human spirit forever from bondage to matter, and opened the way to un-bounded cultural advance. Others just as stoutly maintain that it has made man the slave of the machine, forced all persons into a single mold, placed a premium on servile submission to the mob, introduced a blind worship of quantity, caused the desire for excellence to atrophy, given an ethical sanction to the brutish struggle for material success, destroyed faith in the reign of moral law in the universe, loosened the forces of social disintegration, and set in motion a chain of events destined to consume both civilization and mankind. But this debate, except as it may furnish a truthful analysis of forces and values, can have no practical outcome. If our moralists should unanimously agree that industrial civilization is essentially evil and that we should return at once to the simple society of the past, their combined efforts would be but spray on the armored turrets of a battleship. We cannot turn back. We are at the beginning of an era. New inventions, new discoveries, new thoughts, new experiences, and new hopes have already been woven into the warp and woof of society. Education must come to terms with industrial civilization and discover its tasks in the new age.

Toward a New Civilization*

The peoples of the world today are leaving behind the material forms and agencies of a civilization which in its broad outlines endured for many centuries. This civilization was based on agriculture, animal breeding, handicraft, simple trade, and human energy—a civilization that in its many variants dates practically from the beginning of recorded history. The civilization which our fathers and mothers brought to this continent in the first half of the seventeenth century and molded into a special pattern during the succeeding two hundred years was one of those variants.

We can see clearly that during the last several generations this early civilization of ours has been undergoing a process of profound change and transformation. Today its material foundations are only a memory. Gone are the simple tools with which the versatile farmer tilled his soil, harvested his crops, prepared his food, fashioned his garments, made his utensils, and erected his houses and barns. Gone are the great distances, the dirt roads and trails, the rude carts and sledges, the rafts, flatboats, and sailing ships.

*Education and American Civilization (New York: Teachers College Press, Columbia University, 1952), pp. 127-29, 166-83, 200-1.

Gone are the self-contained rural households and closely knit neighborhoods. Gone also in relative measure are the oxen, horses, and waterwheels, the long years of unrelieved human toil. Gone too in like measure are the local markets, the little stores and shops with their limited wares and services. Gone for most of us is the intimate relation with the elements—with soil, stream, and forest, with wind, rain, and snow, with sun, moon, and stars. So swiftly have these material features of our old agrarian civilization passed away that Lincoln, Grant, and even Cleveland would feel bewildered in the America of today. Indeed many members of the older generation now living experience a sense of bewilderment. And for the most part those of younger years who may feel at home in this new world really do not realize what kind of a world it is. They have experienced no other.

A new civilization is rising in America and throughout the earth—a civilization that is coming to be called industrial—a civilization so strange in its forms, so vast in its reaches, so complex in its patterns, and so mighty in its energies that thoughtful men and women fear that the control of its operations is beyond the powers of its creator. We in America are very closely identified with the rise of this new civilization. In no small measure it is a product of our genius and in some respects is perhaps further on its course here than in any other land. The fact must be emphasized, moreover, that in spite of the common reference to the "industrial revolution" as a limited series of changes in production which took place in England in the eighteenth century and in other countries at later times, the revolution has actually been gathering momentum with every decade. Industrial *civilization* is probably still in its infancy. What it will be like when fully matured, we do not and cannot know. That it will assume, at least for a time, different forms in different societies, among peoples of diverse cultures, may be confidently expected. Moreover, although certain of its broad imperatives and potentialities are already clearly discernible, we may be sure that it will bring many surprises, many challenges, many hazards, many opportunities to mankind.

The uneven advance of industrial civilization, the swift transformation of the material foundations of life and the lag in institutional, ideological, and moral adjustment, have generated the terrifying crises, the wars and depressions, the revolutions and counterrevolutions, of our time. Our world, in both its domestic and its international aspects, is out of joint. Our practical inventiveness, in the words of Stanley Casson, has far outrun our "moral consciousness and social organization." We have one foot in a civilization that is passing away, the other in a civilization that is only beginning to take form. Or to phrase the dilemma more aptly perhaps, as our feet tread the earth of a new world our heads continue to dwell in a world that is gone.

. . . .

In its patterns of organization industrial society is coming to resemble one of its own great machines, with its thousands of separate parts each performing an essential function and articulating with the others in closest harmony. To perceive all of the relationships between workman and workman, labor and management, farm and factory, region and region, industry and commerce, production and distribution, economy and government, work and play, is beyond the powers of a single mind. Even to follow the system of communication through all of its ramifications from the great centers of finance and power down to field and forest and stream, to mine and lathe and fishing boat, and back again, exhausts the imagination. When we add the interplay of social forces, of the hopes and fears and plans of people, of the designs and struggles of organized groups, of corporations, employers, farmers, labor unions, and cooperatives, we confront a condition that would have astonished and frightened the simple farmers and tradesmen of a few generations ago.

This vast system of relationships seems to be extremely sensitive and unstable. Unlike our old agrarian society, with its independent and quasi-independent neighborhoods, industrial society constitutes a single social fabric and is vulnerable as a whole. If it fails to function in any one of many of its innumerable parts, if the outlay for capital goods falls below the danger point, if speculation upsets the delicate financial balance, if purchasing power is insufficient to absorb the goods and services available, it may pass into a condition of general paralysis or crisis—loans are called, shops close their doors, wheels of production stop turning, millions of workmen are thrown on the streets, members of the middle classes consume their savings, farmers endeavor to resurrect the self-contained household of their ancestors, young men and women hesitate to marry and assume the responsibilities of parenthood, and all elements of the population become frightened and seek scapegoats for their troubles. This seems to be what happens when a great economic depression sweeps over the land.

As yet we have contrived no adequate means to operate successfully and smoothly our complex industrial economy. In spite of the repeated testimony of experience, we continue to place our trust in the so-called automatic controls of the free market which prevailed during premachine days. As a matter of fact such controls no longer operate generally in our highly organized economy. Also our experience with depressions demonstrates that the substitutes devised, except during the highly abnormal conditions of war, have been inadequate to keep the economy on an even keel and at a high level of production. Some measure of general planning, direction, and coordination is clearly necessary. Whether this can or should be achieved by a far-reaching fiscal policy, by the direct assumption on the part of existing governmental agencies of responsibility for stabilization, by the creation of some special federal organ to do the job, by the socialization of certain strategically situated branches of the economy, by the establishment of an economic council representative of government, management, labor, and agriculture, by the encouragement of the cooperative movement, or by some combination of these and other proposals, should be the urgent subject of bold debate and experiment. The survival of free institutions undoubtedly waits upon the achievement of success in this venture.

To those who say that general economic planning, coordination, or stabilization of any kind is certain to end in totalitarianism or serfdom, there is a simple rejoinder. If we cannot find an effective substitute for the assumed, but largely mythical, automatic controls and at the same time preserve our essential liberties, then there is no hope for free society in the emerging age. That great dangers will attend any course we may pursue is readily granted. Yet inaction is the most hazardous form of action in this critical epoch. We cannot expect even our democracy, strong as it is, to survive many depressions equal in depth and scope to the one which began in 1929 and continued until the war compelled us to introduce numerous measures of control. Those of us who love freedom should have learned during the past twenty-five years that men and women generally do not prize political liberty above all else. If they are forced to choose between liberty and bread, they will take bread, or perhaps even the promise of bread. We must not permit ourselves to be confronted with this grim and possibly tragic choice. We must find a way of uniting economic stability with political liberty.

This brings the analysis to the most difficult educational problem which the advance of technology has thrust upon us. If we are to manage this highly complex and dynamic society, we shall have to achieve a degree of loyalty to the general welfare that greatly surpasses the demands of the highly individualistic order of our fathers. Some common agreement on social purposes is clearly imperative. How far such agreement is possible or desirable is a question that can be answered only through experience. The same reasoning obviously applies with equal force to the organization of peace in the world. If the nations cannot agree upon and remain loyal to the requisite purposes, they cannot achieve even a fairly durable peace. It is in this area of purposes that the totalitarian state has a great advantage over free society. Dictatorship can impose its will upon a people by the rack, the machine gun, the forced labor camp, and the monolithic direction of all the agencies of propaganda; free society must rely on the slow process of education, political discussion, and general enlightenment to achieve a common mind. Here is one of the greatest challenges confronting our democracy in these troubled and critical times. If we fail to develop concern for the common good at home, we shall lose our liberties; if we fail to develop concern for the common good among the nations, we shall perish.

The burden placed upon human understanding by the complexities of industrial civilization threatens to overwhelm free society. Such a society rests on the assumption that the judgment of common people, of farmers, mechanics, and housewives, is sound and trustworthy. When confronted with the gossamerlike web of relationships reaching out to the borders of the nation and on to the ends of the earth the individual must often experience a sense of utter confusion and helplessness. He must be haunted with the feeling that his mental equipment was not designed to bear the heavy responsibilities of democratic citizenship in such a world. The one hope for human freedom lies in the fullest and most intelligent use of the resources which technology has placed at our disposal—the new forms of communication through which boys and girls, and men and women, might be given knowledge and under-

standing—the press, the moving picture, radio, and television. But
as yet we have given comparatively little serious thought to directing these great engines of enlightenment to such a noble purpose—
possibly because we cannot spare the time from reading our favorite comic, attending our favorite movie theater, listening to our
favorite mystery play, or viewing our favorite wrestling match or
baseball game!

All civilizations of the past, whether despotic or free, have been
alike in one vital respect. They have rested almost wholly or chiefly on the physical energy of men, women, and children. At the
time of the founding of our Republic, through the harnessing of
wind and water, horses and oxen, the power at our disposal was
perhaps twice that of primeval man. Today human energy constitutes but the most insignificant fraction of the total power sustaining our civilization.

Almost two hundred years ago in England, as we have seen, man
succeeded in harnessing the power of steam and forcing this giant
to do his bidding. During subsequent generations, and particularly
since the opening of the twentieth century, the conquest of mechanical power has proceeded swiftly along ever more revolutionary
lines. The age of steam was superseded in large part by the age of
gasoline and electricity, and now we seem to be entering a perfectly fantastic age of atomic power. It should be emphasized, moreover, that the utilization of mechanical energy fails to give the full
measure of our advance. Practical knowledge also is power, knowledge pertaining to the improvement of plants and animals, to the
prevention and cure of disease, to the making of new materials and
substances, to the forecasting, even perhaps to the making, of the
weather. In this sphere progress has been no less impressive than in
the realm of mechanical energy.

The increase of the power factor in human affairs is an achievement of the most profound import. This factor of course has
played a central role in the transformation of our modes of livelihood, our forms of communication, and the general conditions of
life. From earliest times man's standard of living has been limited
by the energy at his command. As long as his chief reliance was on
human muscle, the great masses of people were compelled to struggle from birth to death just to live and reproduce their kind. While
the members of small aristocratic orders enjoyed a measure of leisure and luxury and cultivated both the graces and the vices of

civilization, their privileges were always squeezed out of the toil
and tears of the many. In the age now unfolding men and women
everywhere may have power in almost unlimited abundance. What
they will do with this power is the most critical question now confronting the human race—possibly the most fateful question ever
faced by mankind. This question is in essence the central moral
question of our time.

In 1835, according to Leo Hausleiter, a German engineer and
economist, just as Andrew Jackson was nearing the end of his second term of office, the total capacity of machines in the United
States amounted to only three hundred thousand horsepower. The
corresponding figure for England was the same, for France twenty
thousand, for Germany ten thousand, for the remainder of Europe
ten thousand, and for all other countries of the world combined
ten thousand.[1] Thus one hundred and fifteen years ago the human
race was just beginning to emerge from a condition that had prevailed with but little change for unnumbered centuries.

The increase in the use of mechanical power in the United States
since 1835 is perhaps the best gauge available of the advance of industrial civilization. By 1875 the capacity of our machines reached
a total of seven million eight hundred thousand horsepower, by
1913 one hundred six million, and by 1928 eight hundred ninety-
six million, as compared with three hundred ninety million for the
rest of the world. The extraordinary concentration of this development in America is exaggerated somewhat perhaps by the inclusion in the calculation of the horsepower of our motor vehicles.
But with this factor eliminated the mechanical energy at our disposal almost equaled that of all other countries.

The testimony of the National Resources Committee corrobor-
ates the findings of Hausleiter and brings the record down to 1935.
"The available mechanical power," says the Committee, "has increased from 70 million horsepower in 1900 to over 1 billion in
1935."[2] The committee's tables actually put the figure for the latter year at approximately one billion two hundred thirty million.
In the meantime sixteen more years have passed, years that have
witnessed further technological advances. It seems probable that
the horsepower of our machines now must be at least one and a
half billion.

The meaning of this figure can best be understood if it is converted into its equivalent in human energy. One horsepower is ordi-

narily regarded as equal to the power of twelve men. We may
therefore say that in the form of steam, combustion, and electrical
engines and motors the American people have working for them
today the equivalent of eighteen billion mechanical slaves—almost
nine times the population of the earth. To put the matter even
more simply, these figures mean that for every man, woman, and
child in the United States there are on the average one hundred
twenty mechanical slaves, for every family more than five hundred.
It would seem that, if man ever subsisted solely by the power of
his own muscle, as he did for perhaps a million years, the economic problem in America should now be completely solved and poverty banished forever. No aristocracy or slave-holding class in history ever commanded for its own members such fabulous energies.
According to the Statistical Office of the United Nations, "in
1948, the United States, with 6 percent of the world's population,
produced 43 percent of the world's economic income."[3]

Our increased power to produce cannot be measured fully in
terms of mechanical energy. The advances in chemistry are usher-
ing in a new physical world and radically extending man's dominion over nature. "The present time," said J. D. Bernal seventeen
years ago, "marks the beginning of a transition from the use of materials extracted out of nature to materials constructed by men. If
science can be used to its full capacity, the former will become
relatively less and less important." This same English scientist fore-
sees the time, not far distant, when "we shall enter into a new
world of materials . . . altogether outside our present experience"—
a world in which we can "have combinations of every kind of physical property, lightness, strength, transparency, etc."—a world in
which we shall make "active materials which, like living things, can
change their shape and physical and chemical properties under suit-
able stimuli."[4] The beginnings of this age are already here.

These advances in science and technology have raised our rate of
production far above that of a century ago and have given us the
highest average material standard of living of any large nation in
history. Yet, as a people, we did not comprehend until recently
the full measure of the productive capacity of our economy. A
commentator has observed that the war brought forth two great
surprises: the first was the strength of the Red Army; the second,
the power of the American economy. Certainly our performance
in the struggle against the Axis powers was perfectly fantastic.

Within three years, as more than ten million of our most vigorous young workers were being drawn into the armed services, we increased our industrial productive facilities by nearly one-half and achieved a total national income practically double that of the best peacetime years. In 1944 we reached a level of industrial production not far below that of all the rest of the world combined. At the same time, with the farm population reduced by draft and by migration to the war industries, agricultural production advanced by thirty per cent. This was the first time that our technical knowledge was fully utilized and our productive energies fully released and harnessed.

And the end is not yet. Indeed, as the war entered its last days, mankind entered a new age—an age freighted with such revolutionary possibilities that the mind hesitates to contemplate the perspectives of the future. We are told by the most sober people of technical competence that when the problem of the release and utilization of atomic energy for peaceful purposes is fully mastered, there will open before mankind vistas of power that dwarf the dreams of the most sanguine utopians of the past. All earlier sources of power, we are told, will lose their value. Men will cease mining coal, pumping oil, and building hydroelectric stations. They will turn the wheels of industry, heat their houses, drive their vehicles, sail their ships, fly their airplanes, light their homes and cities, with incredibly tiny amounts of atomic materials. They will travel around the earth at the equator keeping pace with the sun, and perhaps take excursions to the moon and other places beyond their earthly home that they have read about. They will indeed be able to do almost anything they can imagine, if the limiting factor is energy. Also they will realize the ancient dream of the alchemist, of transmuting the baser metals into gold, should they continue their interest in this yellow substance after it has lost its scarcity value. How many years will pass before we enter fully into the new age, we cannot know. Some say twenty years, others fifty, and others a hundred or two. But of this we may be sure, the time will be too brief. We shall not be ready when it comes. The impact on our ways of life will be truly revolutionary, if not catastrophic.

"From the dim beginnings of society, and beyond, down to this very hour," wrote James T. Shotwell some years ago, "war has been used without question and almost without interval."[5]

Man seems to have given quite as much attention to the "improvement" of the instruments of warfare, to making them ever more deadly and terrifying, as to the perfection of the instruments of peace. Today we stand at the crowning point of this long evolution of the military arts. Our present situation may be thus described because we dare not proceed much further along this ancient road. We have already attained such proficiency in the ways of destruction that another world-wide struggle might either utterly destroy civilization everywhere or impose an enduring tyranny on all peoples. Mankind's most fateful hour of decision has struck.

The war recently concluded brought human society to the very edge of the abyss. As we look back now, we wonder how men, women, and children were able to survive its horrors. Even as the struggle proceeded on its course, the resources of science and technology were organized as never before to achieve victory. Building on the experience of the past men created mighty engines of death that literally dwarfed into insignificance everything and anything that had gone before—bombs of high explosive that weighed ten tons, planes that could carry these bombs four thousand miles, rockets that could be guided to their objectives by radio, steel rockets that could be guided to their objectives by radio, steel monsters that could cross rivers and crush houses, flamethrowers that could hurl jellied gasoline with the accuracy of firearms, giant cannons that could strike a target beyond the range of human vision, great battle fleets that could operate continuously thousands of miles from home, and a powerful industry that could pour forth these engines of death in an endless stream. But this is by no means the whole of the story.

As the struggle drew to a close, the curtain was lifted so that we might catch a glimpse of the next war, if man should lack the intelligence, the desire, and the will to establish an enduring peace. The process of destruction was brought to a climax with an atomic bomb whose power of devastation makes obsolete the rival weapons previously employed and brings in a new era of warfare. Even in its infancy this terrible weapon is capable of destroying a great city. What it might become, if permitted to grow to full maturity, only God himself could know. When combined with the resources of electronics and jet propulsion, its possibilities are literally overwhelming. General H. H. Arnold, Chief of the Army Air Forces at the time, predicted in August, 1945, immediately following the capitulation of Japan, that crewless bombers, guided from distant bases, would "home" on their targets and that greatly "improved" atomic bombs would destroy the major cities of an adversary utterly without warning. A scientist is reported as having said that "in the next war it will be possible to destroy any city in the world in twenty minutes." Already, according to report, we have perfected a new giant warplane, the B-36, which is driven by ten engines capable of developing 42,000 horsepower, which has a cruising radius of four thousand miles, and which can carry a bomb load of forty-two tons, four times the capacity of the B-29 that dropped the atomic bomb on Hiroshima. Also we are apparently engaged in the production of "atomic artillery" which will be capable of laying down a barrage of nuclear explosion, and electronic eyes and brains which can see a target and shoot more swiftly and accurately than the most skillful human warrior.

And now we are embarked on the creation of the hydrogen bomb, which in its fully developed form, according to some of its prospective architects, might be capable of exterminating the entire population of the world and making the earth uninhabitable for centuries. Also we hear about the addition of the cosmic ray, deadly diseases, and divers poisonous substances to the arsenals of warring nations. As to what dreadful weapons may lie wholly beyond the veil that mercifully shrouds the future, even distinguished scientists can only speculate. During the present respite, how long or short we know not, man may have his last opportunity to build a lasting peace and make civilization secure on the earth.

The control of these engines of death is one of the most urgent questions facing mankind. They have made war so swift in its flight, so devastating in its impact, so total in its embrace that civilization itself, not in just one country but in all, is in gravest peril. If war is permitted to continue in this little world, the time is almost certain to come when some one nation, exalting the military virtues, guided by a policy of utter ruthlessness, and "getting the jump" on potential adversaries, will subject and hold in bondage all the rest. Once having established complete control over the means of producing these terrible instruments of warfare, over the great chemical, electrical, metallurgical, and machine construction industries of the world, a nation of even modest proportions could rule the earth indefinitely and unchallenged. These great sources of military power must be kept in the hands of those who love justice and are resolved to keep the peace, at least until the virus of war and war-making is purged from the human race. The prospect of the full conquest of atomic energy makes absolutely imperative most vigorous and sustained action toward this end. When that day arrives, as many commentators have observed, all nations standing in the first ranks of scientific advance will be of one size.

The transformation of the weapons of war contains a threat to free institutions at home. The American people must realize that the day of the "long rifle" and the "six-shooter" is past and that the power to take life no longer supports the doctrine that all men are created equal. They must realize also that the second article of our Bill of Rights, which guarantees to all of us the right "to keep and bear arms," has been repealed by the advance of technology. If a single nation could dominate the earth by gaining exclusive possession of tanks, planes, and atomic bombs, a very small minority within a nation could by the same token establish a dictatorship and hold a people in perpetual slavery. Men and women, however brave, cannot rise successfully against machineguns, tanks, and warplanes, to say nothing of atomic bombs and cosmic rays. During the period between the wars the totalitarian states demonstrated under our very eyes the truth of this assertion. If liberty is to endure in America, the people must be ever watchful to control the government and to make sure that the government controls the instruments of warfare.

Our fathers and mothers of the eighteenth century had little more control over the life process than the people of antiquity. They multiplied without restraint, they lived on a monotonous and badly balanced diet, they were mowed down by disease, and they grew old in middle age. Childbirth was fraught with hazard for both mother and infant; smallpox, scarlet fever, measles, and diphtheria were regarded as necessary experiences of childhood; and malaria, tuberculosis, typhoid, yellow fever, and even typhus and Asiatic cholera were looked upon in many places as inevitable visitations of God. The average expectation of life at birth in the most advanced communities and regions was between thirty and thirty-five years.

Achievement of a large measure of control over the forces of human reproduction—one of the most powerful and imperious of natural forces—is laden with fateful consequences. Through knowledge of the sexual process and through invention of contraceptives of ever-increasing potency, the human race has acquired potential dominion over its own increase and is able to flout the ancient injunction to populate the earth. If it so desires, it may commit suicide. The limitation of births has already proceeded so far in America that, in spite of the upsurge of births during the 1940s, a stationary or even declining population may be expected toward the end of the century. A British scientist has described this entire phenomenon as the "invention of sterility." Unless contrary tendencies set in, he suggests that the population of England and Wales, approximately forty-five millions, "would be reduced to less than 6 millions . . . in about 200 years."[6] We are able to determine over a period of time the size and perhaps eventually the quality of our population.

The advance of medical science is one of the glories of our civilization. As a consequence, we live in a world that is far safer from the inroads of disease and ignorance than any that man has ever known. Childbirth has lost its terrors, many deadly distempers have been conquered, numerous irrational fears have been banished, and man's sense of physical security has vastly increased. Bubonic plague, yellow fever, and smallpox have disappeared in America; and typhoid fever and diphtheria have been all but conquered. Other diseases are being brought rapidly under control and yet others are the subject of carefully organized and generously endowed research. Today the average life span is between sixty-five and seventy years. At the same time we must realize that much of our knowledge is not put to use and that we lag far behind what is possible.

The prospect in this realm, as in others, is both promising and terrifying. Unprecedented power is in our possession, and more is on the way. Through knowledge of diet and hygiene and through the general advance of medical science combined with the ability to achieve and maintain an optimum standard of living for all of our people, it is now possible practically to prevent or correct all physical defects, banish most diseases, extend still further the life span, and attain a level of physical well-being beyond the fondest hopes of past ages. The new "wonder drugs" that were put to use with such miraculous results during the war period suggest that we are still in the early stages of knowledge in this field. With further developments in chemistry and the biological sciences the time may not be far distant when man will be able to fashion himself in whatever image may strike his fancy. Given the present level of our ethics and our social organization we can view such a possibility only with deep misgivings. Science and technology have brought mankind far on its way, but toward what destination no one can say with confidence.

From the standpoint of the future of free society here lies one of the most crucial problems of the age. Such a society rests, not only on guarantees of individual security from the violence of mobs and the arbitrary acts of governments, but also on general conditions of life that make possible the development of informed and independent judgment. In our earlier society, with its self-sufficient communities, its open frontiers, its simple face-to-face relations, its wide diffusion of productive property, its local newspapers and meetinghouses, and its relatively unorganized intellectual life, differences in outlook and independence of spirit were generally fostered. The advance of technology has transformed these conditions and greatly reduced the control of the individual over the forces which shape his opinions.

The entire process of mind-forming has become more and more organized, or at least subject to organization. The individual has become increasingly dependent for information, political ideas, and social attitudes on organized education and on the new forms of communication, particularly the daily press, the comic, the movie, and the radio, with television coming swiftly over the horizon. That these new agencies have enormous power has been demonstrated in our time by both advertising companies and totalitarian states. If conducted with a high sense of   public duty, personal integrity, and devotion to truth, they may serve mightily to promote enlightenment, understanding, and good will in our country and throughout the earth. In a world as vast in its reaches, as complicated in its structure, and as dynamic in its movements as ours, they are indispensable to the successful functioning and perhaps the very survival of our democracy.

In many instances, unfortunately, they serve trivial interests, perverted tastes, vested rights, and even the ends of bigotry. Also we know, and to the sorrow of all mankind, that they may be employed to mock and destroy every good thing in the human heritage. When efficiently coordinated under the direction of a ruthless dictatorship, they may be used to keep a whole people in ignorance, force the minds of young and old into a single mold, inculcate bitter hatred and prejudice, lay the psychological foundations of war, and develop a fanatical belief in the unlimited superiority of a party, a class, a race, a nation, or a person. They may be employed to win acceptance of the proposition that black is white, that two plus two equals five, that slavery is freedom, that war is peace, or that any absurdity or falsehood the mind can contrive is true. And when they are combined with the new engines of warfare and the old methods of torture we behold the power base of the contemporary totalitarian states. What these regimes have been able to accomplish in rooting out "dangerous thoughts," in glorifying a self-appointed leader, in propagating doctrines of utter barbarism, and in educating peoples for death is one of the most extraordinary phenomena of this extraordinary age. In his *Nineteen Eighty-Four* George Orwell has drawn an imaginative picture of the totalitarian state in its "perfected" form a generation hence.

Since the war we have witnessed in the Soviet Union a vast demonstration which brings "nineteen eighty-four" very close. It seems that in the final months of the struggle the tiny oligarchy in the Kremlin made one of those unheralded and fateful decisions which the student of Soviet affairs has come to expect. It decided to reverse completely the wartime policy of friendly collaboration with the Western democracies and to revive the policy of revolutionary aggression in the spirit of 1917. This profound shift in policy was followed by a series of powerful decrees by the Central Committee of the All-Union Communist Party which commanded the entire intellectual class to participate actively in the battle with the enemies of Communism at home and abroad. The first of the resolutions was issued on August 14, 1946, and was directed at literary writers and journals. It was followed during the next two years by similar resolutions in the fields of the drama, the cinema, music, science, and humor. They all called for the unbounded glorification of Soviet institutions and the "new Soviet man" and for an equally unbounded denunciation of everything "Western" or "bourgeois." Intellectuals were told that they were "soldiers of Communism" standing in the "front line of fire" and that they should "lash out boldly and attack bourgeois culture which is in a state of emaciation and depravity." Ideological indifference or neutrality was not to be tolerated. "Art for art's sake" was condemned in most scathing terms. A humorist was warned that "his humor over the radio is nothing more than laughter for laughter's sake." Even the circus clowns were given their marching orders. No intellectual was permitted the luxury of silence. The decrees were supported without exception and with violent extravagance by the entire cultural apparatus and by all the agencies of mass communication.

Democracy everywhere rests on the freedom of the individual mind. To preserve such freedom in the present epoch is one of our most difficult and urgent tasks. We must realize that the elements in the equation of human liberty have been profoundly altered by the advance of science and technology. The problem is made the more critical and disturbing by the trend toward monopoly in the control of the media of mass communication.

. . . .

This is not to say that the press, the radio, the moving picture, and television do not serve the cause of enlightenment and understanding. At their best they are truly magnificent; without them we would be wholly lost.

Yet no thoughtful person can view with complacency their total impact upon the minds of our people. Often they are directed by narrow partisan motives or by purely business considerations of material profit and loss. In considerable part they play the role of the "circus" during the decadent period of ancient Rome, stultifying and debauching the mind, corrupting and degrading the processes of thought. Let anyone who takes exception to this indictment listen to the radio broadcast for twenty-four hours over any one of the great networks and note the amount of drivel, misrepresentation, and downright falsehood included in the programs. The advertisement of nostrums of doubtful worth is associated with the names of distinguished commentators and the findings of "science." Much of the "output" of Hollywood can serve only as a form of vulgar escape from the realities of the contemporary world. While all of these agencies may serve to modify profoundly our sex mores and to take our minds off our troubles, they can scarcely be credited with helping us to bridge the great gulf which runs through our civilization. At any rate they are not employing their matchless resources to cultivate the virtues and develop the understandings necessary for the survival of free institutions.

The schools lag far behind the march of events. Although the service they render in their present form is indispensable to the functioning of our society, they fall well below the requirements of the age. In their programs they reveal little gras   of the character of industrial civilization, except in its more superficial aspects. They teach the findings of science, but fail to instill the spirit of science or to convey an understanding of what science is doing to the world and human institutions. They transmit the words of the tradition of human freedom, but fail to arouse concern or to apply old meanings to new conditions. They encourage the development of egoistic and competitive impulses suited perhaps to the society of yesterday, but fail to foster effectively the social and cooperative tendencies, the devotion to the general welfare necessary for successful living in the society of today. They do a magnificent job in preparing for war when the occasion demands it, but they have yet to formulate a bold and imaginative program to build a peaceful world. They have vast potentialities that remain undeveloped. They lack a generous and realistic conception of their task. They are without vision.

5 The Challenges of Totalitarianism and the Promise of Democracy

Democracy in Retreat*

A generation ago in America an order of society and government called democracy seemed triumphant. The wisdom, beneficence, and perdurance of this order were generally accepted as axiomatic. The people of the United States took pride in the characterization of their country as the "great democracy of the West" and nourished the conviction that for generations they had been leading mankind in the long struggle for popular liberty and justice. They believed firmly that the twentieth century would witness the spread of democratic ideas, values, and institutions throughout the world. To them the principle of autocracy was a barbaric survival from the dark ages, at last in full retreat before the rising tide of popular enlightenment and destined soon to be relegated to the limbo of history.

To the discerning eye, to be sure, somber clouds, presaging coming storms, appeared above the social horizon. At home, the contest between capital and labor would burst forth now and then into bloody conflict—bitter and ruthless—to reveal deep differences bearing the seed of eventual civil strife. Abroad, the great nations, engaged in a struggle for markets, raw materials, colonies, and spheres of influence, had entered upon a war of diplomatic maneuver and military armament which with every year became

*The Prospects of American Democracy (New York: John Co., 1938), pp. 1-7.

more strained and savage. And in all modern nations minority parties, organizations, and movements, born of industrial capitalism, were demanding profound changes in the social structure and even preaching the doctrines of violent revolution.

Shortly before his death in 1910, William Graham Sumner, seeing these portents and being aware of fundamental changes in society already far advanced, made a striking observation and prophecy. "I have lived through the best period of this country's history," he said. "The next generations are going to see war and social calamities. I am glad I don't have to live on into them."[1] Others, both scholars and men of affairs, foresaw in broad outline the coming crisis in American and world civilization; but the vast majority of people, then as in times past, stood on the threshold of great convulsions and had not the slightest inkling of the forces stirring beneath their feet—forces which within a few years would alter the whole aspect of their lives and bring pain, privation, disillusionment, desperation, and death to millions throughout the world. To the ordinary middle-class American, socialism was an annoying curiosity, communism but a word in the dictionary; while the term fascism was yet to be coined. The class struggle, the red flag, the hammer and sickle, the swastika, the totalitarian state held for him little or no social significance. He passed from election to election much as he passed from one baseball season to the next. Not that bitter political battles were unknown to him. The Civil War was vividly recalled to his mind every Memorial Day. But he felt that at last the rules of the game had been firmly established and that even the stars in their courses were fighting on the side of democracy and the democratic process. He would have agreed with the following estimate with which Professor J. B. Bury in 1913 concluded his study of the history of freedom of thought: "The struggle of reason against authority has ended in what appears now to be a decisive and permanent victory for liberty. In the most civilized and progressive countries, freedom of discussion is recognized as a fundamental principle."[2]

Today the outlook is radically changed. No friend of free institutions can view the present situation in the nation and the world with equanimity. Since the Great War one country after another has taken the road to revolution and dictatorship; and no country, not even the oldest of the democracies, has wholly escaped the virus. These new autocracies, seizing power by diverse methods, have suspended civil liberties and rule by the radio and the machine gun. Having established their special orthodoxies, they organize priesthoods of the new political faiths, forge into a single instrument all the agencies of propaganda, set up rigorous border patrols against the entrance of "dangerous ideas and persons," and seek in every way to mold the minds of their respective peoples. Where propaganda fails, they have recourse to espionage, secret police, torture, concentration camps, firing squads, sadistic orgies, and assassinations. At the same time piracy returns to the seas, powerful nations wage undeclared war on defenseless peoples, rival systems of provocation carry on a deadly struggle under the cloak of peaceful professions, and the moral foundations of international order are condemned and mocked. Only too well authenticated is the doubt, expressed by Lytton Strachey in his review of Professor Bury's book at the time of its publication, that the long struggle for liberty of thought had been crowned with final success during the reign of Queen Victoria: "Well, that is very nice, very nice indeed—if it is true. But, after all, can we be quite so sure that it *is* true? Is it really credible that the human race should have got along so far as that? That such deeply rooted instincts as the love of persecution and the hatred of heterodoxies should have been dissipated into thin air by the charms of philosophers and the common sense of that remarkable period the nineteenth century?"[3]

The attack upon democracy comes from both left and right. Under the banners of communism a dictatorship is set up, paradoxically, in the name of democracy—a "dictatorship of the proletariat" which in actual practice becomes a dictatorship first of a party that claims to represent the proletariat and then of a handful of men who claim to represent the party. The object and justification of the dictatorship, according to the theory, is the establishment ultimately of the most complete democracy in history—a society without economic classes in which the exploitation of man by man will be abolished, all races and peoples will live in peace and harmony, and mankind generally will achieve maturity and enter upon its rightful inheritance. The repudiation of democracy is said to be temporary and partial, a hard necessity forced upon the present epoch by an irreconcilable and irrepressible conflict of classes. But whatever the doctrine the fact is that free political institutions are repudiated and a regime of minority rule and strict censorship of speech and thought inaugurated.

In the case of fascism the repudiation of democracy is complete and uncompromising. The concept of equality, whether applied to races or to individuals, is scorned and rejected, not merely because it is unattainable, but because it is contrary to the spirit that rules the universe. Inequality being everywhere the law of nature, the strong are urged to mastery, even as the weak are admonished to practice submission. For the strong to refuse to exercise fully the rights attached to power would be to engage in the grossest immorality, to violate the purpose of creation, to commit the unpardonable sin of history. This theme constitutes the core of the philosophical writings of the fascist leaders and permeates the program of public education. In a guide prepared by Wilhelm Stuckart for the German teacher of history the following doctrine is propagated repeatedly: "The experience of history and the findings of racial science teach us that Democracy has always been the political form of the racial decline of a creative people."[4]

There is of course nothing novel in the struggle between democracy and autocracy. The former has had to contend with the latter wherever and whenever it has appeared in human history. The novel and disturbing feature of the present situation is the fact that the contemporary dictator actually achieves power through an appeal to the broad masses of the population. Thus in Germany, a nation justly renowned for its cultural achievements and for the high intellectual level of its people, Hitler succeeded in building up the most powerful political party in the Reich, took over the reins of government by constitutional means, and immediately destroyed the republic. The German people seem to have abdicated deliberately in favor of a dictator who during his career had given every evidence of being arbitrary, ruthless, brutal, and mad. Democracy, having lost its *élan vital*, its desire to live, its belief in itself, presumably committed suicide. At the present juncture in world affairs it seems that a considerable proportion of men and women have neither the desire nor the will to govern themselves. They prefer to prostrate both body and soul before a leader to whom they attach divine or quasi-divine attributes and to submerge their persons in a movement which they do not understand but which they hope will prove beneficent. In any country today, if circumstances should become favorable, it would be possible to secure wide popular support for the overthrow of popular rule.

The extraordinary careers of Huey Long and Father Coughlin, not to mention others, suggest that this could happen even in the greatest and most celebrated of the democracies.

The contemporary attack upon democracy is militant and inspired. It has assumed the features of a crusading faith. It has formulated an interpretation of history which provides moral support for the spirit of unabashed aggression and destroys utterly the foundations for the promotion of peace and understanding among the nations. Indeed it rejects peace as an ideal and glorifies war and conquest, raising imperialistic adventure to the level of the paramount national virtue. "For Fascism," writes Mussolini in a considered article in the *Enciclopedia Italiana*, "the growth of empire, that is to say the expansion of the nation, is an essential manifestation of vitality, and its opposite a sign of decadence. Peoples who are rising, or rising again after a period of decadence, are always imperialistic: any renunciation is a sign of decay and death."[5] And the spirit of fascism, in both its domestic and its international implications, is by no means absent from the United States. During the present period of distress there has been talk of substituting bullets for ballots and not a little resort to violence in the settlement of disputes.

In the face of the world-wide assault upon its ideas, values, and institutions, democracy tends either to retreat or to assume a defensive role. As the democratically elected government of Spain fights for its life against the aggressive designs and even invading armies of two fascist states, officially supported and blessed by the hierarchy of the most powerful authoritarian ecclesiastical organization in the contemporary world, the great democracies, torn by internal doubts and conflicts, stand idly by and even acquiesce in the subversion of international law calculated to weaken the Spanish democracy. These events lend support to the paradoxical observation of H. N. Brailsford that the democratic governments of Western Europe, had they not been democracies, "might have saved Democracy in Germany with comparative ease."[6] It may later be added that, if they had not been democracies they might have saved democracy within their own borders without difficulty.

In their theoretical advocacy the friends of democracy adopt a defensive or even an apologetic tone. The best they can say is that while democracy is not as good as it should be, it is not as bad as it might be. Cataloguing and commending its merits, conceding and lamenting its defects, and conscientiously balancing argument

against argument, they arrive at the tentative conclusion that democracy is a trifle superior to any rival order of society and life,
as if diverse social systems were readily commensurable. Moreover,
in an age when great choices have to be made, when positive and
determined social action has to be taken, democracy is denomi-
nated the middle way. Obviously if such a conception of democracy should prevail, its worst enemies could ask for nothing better.
It would become a deceptive haven for the timid and the vacilla-
ting, while the bolder spirits would enroll under banners repre-
senting positive and challenging philosophies and programs. As a
matter of fact, democracy is by no means a middle way between
extremes, lacking substance of its own and defined in terms of its
opponents. It is another way—unique, radical, revolutionary—the
most adventurous way that man has ever taken—a way beset with
difficulties and demanding the fullest possible development of the
powers of the race.

The Totalitarian Mind*

We must avoid, as we would avoid the plague, for that is precisely
what it is to a free society—"the totalitarian mind." While elements
of this mind are as old as human history, the full conception, as we
know it, is of recent origin and is moulded by the forces of industrial society. It has been forged in this century by the victorious
advances of Russian Communism, Italian Fascism, and German
National Socialism. That the latter two were launched ostensibly
to combat the first should be illuminating to the student of contemporary events in our own society. As we all know, the totalitarian scourge brought on the Second World War, and today in its
Communist variant holds in bondage over one-third of the human
race, penetrates every society on the planet, and is committed to
the destruction of the spirit of freedom throughout the earth.

The major features of the totalitarian mind are written large in
the history of this tragic epoch. Although there are differences between leaders and followers, the following characteristics would
seem to give us a fairly trustworthy portrait of this type of mind,
whether Communist, Fascist, or Nazi:

*Education and the Foundations of Human Freedom (Pittsburgh: University
of Pittsburgh Press, 1963), pp. 94-99.

1. The totalitarian regards as right whatever advances his cause, or whatever he thinks will advance his cause. He completely subordinates means to ends. In the words of the notorious "Catechism of a Revolutionist" formulated in Russia in the 1860s by Michael Bakunin or Sergei Nechaiev or by both, "to him whatever aids the triumph of the revolution is ethical; everything that hinders it is unethical and criminal."

2. He repudiates the idea of objective truth and defines as truth whatever aids his cause. His ethics are the ethics of war. One need only look for confirmation in Soviet histories and Nazi anthropologies. Moreover, in his struggle for power he will promise anything and everything calculated to arouse discontent and to attract the discontented.

3. He repudiates the idea of human dignity. He is utterly ruthless and is prepared to liquidate families, classes, nations, or races. And he may do these things in the name of liberty, equality, and fraternity.

4. He glorifies the role of violence in both word and deed in history. He speaks incessantly of struggle, battle, and war, even as he proclaims his dedication to peace. He deliberately arouses and exploits prejudices, hatreds, and passions. He thinks in terms of castor oil, slippery elm clubs, forced labor camps, machine guns, and execution chambers.

5. He outlaws freedom of speech and thought, and even freedom of silence. He labels all criticism as treason and prohibits the formation of rival parties and organizations. He is guided by the following principle contained in a Russian revolutionary proclamation of 1862: "Remember that whoever is not with us is against us, that whoever is against us is our enemy, and that an enemy must be exterminated by all possible means."

6. He seeks to control all agencies and processes for the molding and informing of the minds of both young and old. In this effort he overlooks nothing from the school and the theatre to the calendar and the circus. His motto is "Control everything."

7. He performs all of his acts in the name of his class, his people, his nation, or his race—in the name of patriotism, public safety, or love of "all progressive mankind." And he does this without consulting those in whose name he speaks.

8. He is certain of the rightness of his policies and the grandeur of his mission in history, whether he appeals to the authority of

"blood" or the "laws of social development," which he alone understands.

9. He rejects completely the conception of the higher law—the law above the state. He rejects the right of conscience, for he is God.

This totalitarian mind has penetrated our society. It is found, of course, in its purest form perhaps in the Communist Party. But, as an expression of the dialectical process in history, it is found also in some individuals and organizations which would combat the Communist menace by appropriating its morals and methods and by thus destroying our own most precious freedoms. The study of totalitarianism and the totalitarian mind should constitute an essential element in education for human freedom.

Democracy as a Goal*

In *The Epic of America* James Truslow Adams contends that our chief contribution to the heritage of the race lies not in the field of science, or religion, or literature, or art but rather in the creation of what he calls the "American Dream"—a vision of a society in which the lot of the common man will be made easier and his life enriched and ennobled. If this vision has been a moving force in our history, as I believe it has, why should we not set ourselves the task of revitalizing and reconstituting it? This would seem to be the great need of our age, both in the realm of education and in the sphere of public life, because men must have something for which to live. Agnosticism, skepticism, or even experimentalism, unless the last is made flesh through the formulation of some positive social program, constitutes an extremely meager spiritual diet for any people. A small band of intellectuals, a queer breed of men at best, may be satisfied with such a spare ration, particularly if they lead the sheltered life common to their class; but the masses, I am sure, will always demand something more solid and substantial. Ordinary men and women crave a tangible purpose towards which to strive and which lends richness and dignity and meaning to life. I would consequently like to see our profession

*Dare the School Build a New Social Order? (Carbondale: Southern Illinois University Press, 1978), pp. 35-52 [Arno Press ed., pp. 38-56].

come to grips with the problem of creating a tradition that has
roots in American soil, is in harmony with the spirit of the age,
recognizes the facts of industrialism, appeals to the most profound
impulses of our people, and takes into account the emergence of a
world society.[7]

The ideal foundations on which we must build are easily discernible. Until recently the very word America has been synony-
mous throughout the world with democracy and symbolic to the
oppressed classes of all lands of hope and opportunity. Child of
the revolutionary ideas and impulses of the eighteenth century,
the American nation became the embodiment of bold social experimentation and a champion of the power of environment to develop the capacities and redeem the souls of common men and
women. And as her stature grew, her lengthening shadow reached
to the four corners of the earth and everywhere impelled the human will to rebel against ancient wrongs. Here undoubtedly is the
finest jewel in our heritage and the thing that is most worthy of
preservation. If America should lose her honest devotion to democracy, or if she should lose her revolutionary temper, she will
no longer be America. In that day, if it has not already arrived, her
spirit will have fled and she will be known merely as the richest
and most powerful of the nations. If America is not to be false to
the promise of her youth, she must do more than simply perpetu-
ate the democratic ideal of human relationships: she must make
an intelligent and determined effort to fulfill it. The democracy of
the past was the chance fruit of a strange conjunction of forces on
the new continent; the democracy of the future can only be the
intended offspring of the union of human reason, purpose, and
will. The conscious and deliberate achievement of democracy under novel circumstances is the task of our generation.

Democracy of course should not be identified with political
forms and functions—with the federal constitution, the popular
election of officials, or the practice of universal suffrage. To think
in such terms is to confuse the entire issue, as it has been confused
in the minds of the masses for generations. The most genuine expression of democracy in the United States has little to do with
our political institutions: it is a sentiment with respect to the
moral equality of men: it is an aspiration towards a society in
which this sentiment will find complete fulfillment. A society fashioned in harmony with the American democratic tradition would

combat all forces tending to produce social distinctions and classes; repress every form of privilege and economic parasitism; manifest a tender regard for the weak, the ignorant, and the unfortunate; place the heavier and more onerous social burdens on the backs of the strong; glory in every triumph of man in his timeless urge to express himself and to make the world more habitable; exalt human labor of hand and brain as the creator of all wealth and culture; provide adequate material and spiritual rewards for every kind of socially useful work; strive for genuine equality of opportunity among all races, sects, and occupations; regard as paramount the abiding interests of the great masses of the people; direct the powers of government to the elevation and the refinement of the life of the common man; transform or destroy all conventions, institutions, and special groups inimical to the underlying principles of democracy; and finally be prepared as a last resort, in either the defense or the realization of this purpose, to follow the method of revolution. Although these ideals have never been realized or perhaps even fully accepted anywhere in the United States and have always had to struggle for existence with contrary forces, they nevertheless have authentic roots in the past. They are the values for which America has stood before the world during most of her history and with which the American people have loved best to associate their country. Their power and authority are clearly revealed in the fact that selfish interests, when grasping for some special privilege, commonly wheedle and sway the masses by repeating the words and kneeling before the emblems of the democratic heritage.

It is becoming increasingly clear, however, that this tradition, if its spirit is to survive, will have to be reconstituted in the light of the great social trends of the age in which we live. Our democratic heritage was largely a product of the frontier, free land, and a simple agrarian order. Today a new and strange and closely integrated industrial economy is rapidly sweeping over the world. Although some of us in our more sentimental moments talk wistfully of retiring into the more tranquil society of the past, we could scarcely induce many of our fellow citizens to accompany us. Even the most hostile critics of industrialism would like to take with them in their retirement a few such fruits of the machine as electricity, telephones, automobiles, modern plumbing, and various labor-saving devices, or at least be assured of an abundant supply of slaves or docile and inexpensive servants. But all such talk is the most idle chatter. For better or for worse we must take industrial civilization as an enduring fact: already we have become parasitic on its institutions and products. The hands of the clock cannot be turned back.

If we accept industrialism, as we must, we are then compelled to face without equivocation the most profound issue which this new order of society has raised and settle that issue in terms of the genius of our people—the issue of the control of the machine. In whose interests and for what purposes are the vast material riches, the unrivaled industrial equipment, and the science and technology of the nation to be used? In the light of our democratic tradition there can be but one answer to the question: all of these resources must be dedicated to the promotion of the welfare of the great masses of the people. Even the classes in our society that perpetually violate this principle are compelled by the force of public opinion to pay lip-service to it and to defend their actions in its terms. No body of men, however powerful, would dare openly to flout it. Since the opening of the century the great corporations have even found it necessary to establish publicity departments or to employ extremely able men as public relations counselors in order to persuade the populace that regardless of appearances they are lovers of democracy and devoted servants of the people. In this they have been remarkably successful, at least until the coming of the great depression. For during the past generation there have been few things in America that could not be bought at a price.

If the benefits of industrialism are to accrue fully to the people, this deception must be exposed. If the machine is to serve all, and serve all equally, it cannot be the property of the few. To ask these few to have regard for the common weal, particularly when under the competitive system they are forced always to think first of themselves or perish, is to put too great a strain on human nature. With the present concentration of economic power in the hands of a small class, a condition that is likely to get worse before it gets better, the survival or development of a society that could in any sense be called democratic is unthinkable. The hypocrisy which is so characteristic of our public life today is due primarily to our failure to acknowledge the fairly obvious fact that America is the scene of an irreconcilable conflict between two opposing forces. On the one side is the democratic tradition inherited from the past;

on the other is a system of economic arrangements which increasingly partakes of the nature of industrial feudalism. Both of these forces cannot survive: one or the other must give way. Unless the democratic tradition is able to organize and conduct a successful attack on the economic system, its complete destruction is inevitable.

If democracy is to survive, it must seek a new economic foundation. Our traditional democracy rested upon small-scale production in both agriculture and industry and a rather general diffusion of the rights of property in capital and natural resources. The driving force at the root of this condition, as we have seen, was the frontier and free land. With the closing of the frontier, the exhaustion of free land, the growth of population, and the coming of large-scale production, the basis of ownership was transformed. If property rights are to be diffused in industrial society, natural resources and all important forms of capital will have to be collectively owned. Obviously every citizen cannot hold title to a mine, a factory, a railroad, a department store, or even a thoroughly mechanized farm. This clearly means that, if democracy is to survive in the United States, it must abandon its individualistic affiliations in the sphere of economics. What precise form a democratic society will take in the age of science and the machine, we cannot know with any assurance today. We must, however, insist on two things: first, that technology be released from the fetters and the domination of every type of special privilege; and, second, that the resulting system of production and distribution be made to serve directly the masses of the people. Within these limits, as I see it, our democratic tradition must of necessity evolve and gradually assume an essentially collectivistic pattern. The only conceivable alternative is the abandonment of the last vestige of democracy and the frank adoption of some modern form of feudalism.

The important point is that fundamental changes in the economic system are imperative. Whatever services historic capitalism may have rendered in the past, and they have been many, its days are numbered. With its deification of the principle of selfishness, its exaltation of the profit motive, its reliance upon the forces of competition, and its placing of property above human rights, it will either have to be displaced altogether or changed so radically in form and spirit that its identity will be completely lost. In view of the fact that the urge for private gain tends to debase everything that it touches, whether business, recreation, religion, art, or friendship, the indictment against capitalism has commonly been made on moral grounds. But today the indictment can be drawn in other terms.

Capitalism is proving itself weak at the very point where its champions have thought it impregnable. It is failing to meet the pragmatic test; it no longer works; it is unable even to organize and maintain production. In its present form capitalism is not only cruel and inhuman; it is also wasteful and inefficient. It has exploited our natural resources without the slightest regard for the future needs of our society; it has forced technology to serve the interests of the few rather than the many; it has chained the engineer to the vagaries and inequities of the price system; it has plunged the great nations of the earth into a succession of wars ever more devastating and catastrophic in character; and only recently it has brought on a world crisis of such dimensions that the entire economic order is paralyzed and millions of men in all the great industrial countries are deprived of the means of livelihood. The growth of science and technology has carried us into a new age where ignorance must be replaced by knowledge, competition by cooperation, trust in providence by careful planning, and private capitalism by some form of socialized economy.

Already the individualism of the pioneer and the farmer, produced by free land, great distances, economic independence, and a largely self-sustaining family economy, is without solid foundation in either agriculture or industry. Free land has long since disappeared. Great distances have been shortened immeasurably by invention. Economic independence survives only in the traditions of our people. Self-sustaining family economy has been swallowed up in a vast society which even refuses to halt before the boundaries of nations. Already we live in an economy which in its functions is fundamentally cooperative. There remains the task of reconstructing our economic institutions and of reformulating our social ideals so that they may be in harmony with the underlying facts of life. The man who would live unto himself alone must retire from the modern world. The day of individualism in the production and distribution of goods is gone. The fact cannot be overemphasized that choice is no longer between individualism and collectivism. It is rather between two forms of collectivism: the one essentially democratic, the other feudal in spirit; the one devoted to the interests of the people, the other to the interests of a privileged class.

The objection is of course raised at once that a planned, coordinated, and socialized economy, managed in the interests of the people, would involve severe restrictions on personal freedom. Undoubtedly in such an economy the individual would not be permitted to do many things that he has customarily done in the past. He would not be permitted to carve a fortune out of the natural resources of the nation, to organize a business purely for the purpose of making money, to build a new factory or railroad whenever and wherever he pleased, to throw the economic system out of gear for the protection of his own private interests, to amass or to attempt to amass great riches by the corruption of the political life, the control of the organs of opinion, the manipulation of the financial machinery, the purchase of brains and knowledge, or the exploitation of ignorance, frailty, and misfortune. In exchange for such privileges as these, which only the few could ever enjoy, we would secure the complete and uninterrupted functioning of the productive system and thus lay the foundations for a measure of freedom for the many that mankind has never known in the past. Freedom without a secure economic foundation is only a word: in our society it may be freedom to beg, steal, or starve. The right to vote, if it cannot be made to insure the right to work, is but an empty bauble. Indeed it may be less than a bauble: it may serve to drug and dull the senses of the masses. Today only the members of the plutocracy are really free, and even in their case freedom is rather precarious. If all of us could be assured of material security and abundance, we would be released from economic worries and our energies liberated to grapple with the central problems of cultural advance.

Under existing conditions, however, no champion of the democratic way of life can view the future with equanimity. If democracy is to be achieved in the industrial age, powerful classes must be persuaded to surrender their privileges, and institutions deeply rooted in popular prejudice will have to be radically modified or abolished. And according to the historical record, this process has commonly been attended by bitter struggle and even bloodshed. Ruling classes never surrender their privileges voluntarily. Rather do they cling to what they have been accustomed to regard as their rights, even though the heavens fall. Men customarily defend their

property, however it may have been acquired, as tenaciously as the
proverbial mother defends her young. There is little evidence from
the pages of American history to support us in the hope that we
may adjust our difficulties through the method of sweetness and
light. Since the settlement of the first colonists along the Atlantic
seaboard we have practiced and become inured to violence. This is
peculiarly true wherever and whenever property rights, actual or
potential, have been involved. Consider the pitiless extermination
of the Indian tribes and the internecine strife over the issue of
human slavery. Consider the long reign of violence in industry,
from the days of the Molly Maguires in the seventies down to the
strikes in the mining regions of Kentucky today. Also let those,
whose memories reach back a dozen years, recall the ruthlessness
with which the privileged classes put down every expression of
economic or political dissent during the period immediately following the World War. When property is threatened, constitutional
guarantees are but scraps of paper and even the courts and the
churches, with occasional exceptions, rush to the support of privilege and vested interest.

This is a dark picture. If we look at the future through the eyes
of the past, we find little reason for optimism. If there is to be no
break in our tradition of violence, if a bold and realistic program
of education is not forthcoming, we can only anticipate a struggle
of increasing bitterness terminating in revolution and disaster. And
yet, as regards the question of property, the present situation has
no historical parallel. In earlier paragraphs I have pointed to the
possibility of completely disposing of the economic problem. For
the first time in history we are able to produce all the goods and
services that our people can consume. The justification, or at least
the rational basis, of the age-long struggle for property has been
removed. This situation gives to teachers an opportunity and a responsibility unique in the annals of education.

In an economy of scarcity, where the population always tends
to outstrip the food supply, any attempt to change radically the
rules of the game must inevitably lead to trial by the sword. But
in an economy of plenty, which the growth of technology has
made entirely possible, the conditions are fundamentally altered.
It is natural and understandable for men to fight when there is
scarcity, whether it be over air, water, food, or women. For them
to fight over the material goods of life in America today is sheer

insanity. Through the courageous and intelligent reconstruction of their economic institutions they could all obtain, not only physical security, but also the luxuries of life and as much leisure as men could ever learn to enjoy. For those who take delight in combat, ample provision for strife could of course be made; but the more cruel aspects of the human struggle would be considerably softened. As the possibilities in our society begin to dawn upon us, we are all, I think, growing increasingly weary of the brutalities, and stupidities, the hypocrisies, and the gross inanities of contemporay life. We have a haunting feeling that we were born for better things and that the nation itself is falling far short of its powers. The fact that other groups refuse to deal boldly and realistically with the present situation does not justify the teachers of the country in their customary policy of hesitation and equivocation. The times are literally crying for a new vision of American destiny. The teaching profession, or at least its progressive elements, should eagerly grasp the opportunity which the fates have placed in their hands.

Such a vision of what America might become in the industrial age I would introduce into our schools as the supreme imposition, but one to which our children are entitled—a priceless legacy which it should be the first concern of our profession to fashion and bequeath. The objection will of course be raised that this is asking teachers to assume unprecedented social responsibilities. But we live in difficult and dangerous times—times when precedents lose their significance. If we are content to remain where all is safe and quiet and serene, we shall dedicate ourselves, as teachers have commonly done in the past, to a role of futility, if not of positive social reaction. Neutrality with respect to the great issues that agitate society, while perhaps theoretically possible, is practically tantamount to giving support to the forces of conservatism. As Justice Holmes has candidly said in his essay on Natural Law, "we all, whether we know it or not, are fighting to make the kind of world that we should like." If neutrality is impossible even in the dispensation of justice, whose emblem is blindfolded goddess, how is it to be achieved in education? To ask the question is to answer it.

To refuse to face the task of creating a vision of a future America immeasurably more just and noble and beautiful than the America of today is to evade the most crucial, difficult, and important educational task. Until we have assumed this responsibility we are scarcely justified in opposing and mocking the efforts of so-called patriotic societies to introduce into the schools a tradition which, though narrow and unenlightened, nevertheless represents an honest attempt to meet a profound social and educational need. Only when we have fashioned a finer and more authentic vision than they will we be fully justified in our opposition to their efforts. Only they will we have discharged the age-long obligation which the older generation owes to the younger and which no amount of sophistry can obscure. Only through such a legacy of spiritual values will our children be enabled to find their place in the world, be lifted out of the present morass of moral indifference, be liberated from the senseless struggle for material success, and be challenged to high endeavor and achievement. And only thus will we as a people put ourselves on the road to the expression of our peculiar genius and to the making of our special contribution to the cultural heritage of the race.

6 The American Teacher

Teachers as Shapers of Culture*

In the great battle of ideas and values precipitated by the advance
of industrial civilization the teachers of the country are inevitably
and intimately involved. They cannot stand apart and at the same
time discharge their professional obligations. This is due to the
fact that they are guardians of childhood, bearers of culture, and,
presumably, loyal servants of the masses of the people. These three
considerations compel the teachers to action.

As guardians of childhood teachers cannot be indifferent to the
operation of social institutions. In normal times they are keenly
aware of the injustice and the misery wrought by the existing economic system. They know that capitalism, with its extremes of
poverty and riches and its moral degradation of millions, makes an
empty farce of our democratic professions and dooms multitudes
of children to lives of severe privation. They know that these children will have to forego, not only the luxuries which are literally
showered upon their more fortunate brothers and sisters born to
wealth and privilege, but even those things demanded by the laws
of physical and mental health. Teachers can never be reconciled to
a social order that even in days of "prosperity" needlessly violates
the deepest loyalties of their calling. Then in years of depression
they see additional millions of boys and girls deprived of their
social birthright, denied the most elementary material and cultural
necessities, and crippled beyond hope of redemption in body,

*A Call to the Teachers of America (New York: John Day Co., 1933), pp.
18-26.

mind, and spirit. They see the youth of the nation bewildered by the deep chasm separating precept from reality and embittered as they beat vainly against the closed doors of occupational opportunity. They even see that no defensible theory of education can be practiced successfully in contemporary society. Consequently, if they are but interested in the lives of children—the central responsibility with which they are charged by the state—they must work boldly and without ceasing for a better social order.

Teachers are also bearers of culture. In their own persons, in their selection of the materials of instruction, in their organization of the life of the school, in their connections with the community, they must give expression to some set of values. Education itself is essentially a process of cultural transmission and transformation. It therefore cannot be neutral toward the great issues of life and destiny without becoming completely formalized and losing all contact with the world. If the school is to live, some vital and growing tradition must provide it with nourishment, some conception of worth must course through and animate and integrate its organs and tissues. This is clearly sensed by the American people in their insistence that the young be reared on the democratic ideal. But the difficulty arises out of the fact, already noted, that the ideal has lost much of its meaning and requires reformulation in the light of vastly changed conditions. *To teach the ideal in its historic form, without the illumination that comes from an effort to apply it to contemporary society, is an extreme instance of intellectual dishonesty. It constitutes an attempt to educate the youth for life in a world that does not exist. Teachers therefore cannot evade the responsibility of participating actively in the task of reconstituting the democratic tradition and of thus working positively toward a new society.* The simple discharge of their professional duties leaves to them no alternative.

Finally, attention should be directed to the fact that teachers are at the same time the loyal servants and the spiritual leaders of the masses of the people. This does not mean, however, as some have maintained, that teachers are to regard themselves as mere tools in the hands of the state; nor does it mean that they are constrained to defend the existing social system and serve the interests of the dominant class. To do either would be a gross violation of trust. Such arguments are purely legalistic or mechanistic in character and fail utterly to express the nature of the educative and

social processes. Even the taxpayers have no special claim on the
schools; they are but the tax collectors of society; ultimately
school revenue comes from all who labor by hand or brain. This
the teachers should never forget. Their loyalty therefore goes to
the great body of the laboring population—to the farmers, the industrial workers, and the other members of the producing classes
of the nation. They owe nothing to the present economic system,
except to improve it; they owe nothing to any privileged caste, except to strip it of its privileges. Their sole duty is to guard and promote the widest and most permanent interests of society. Though
seeking alliance from time to time with those groups that can be
relied upon to work for the establishment of a genuine democracy,
they can take dictation from none. They must always be in a position to place their faith, their intelligence, their idealistic fervor,
and not merely their professional skill, at the service of the masses
of the people. Today, when life seems so freighted with possibilities, these broader responsibilities should receive the most earnest
consideration of teachers. As never before in their history they
should recognize their social obligations and be prepared to participate in the struggles of the day.

If the teachers are to play a positive and creative role in building a better social order, indeed if they are not to march in the
ranks of economic, political, and cultural reaction, they will have
to emancipate themselves completely from the domination of the
business interests of the nation, cease cultivating the manners and
associations of bankers and promotion agents, repudiate utterly
the ideal of material success as the goal of education, abandon the
smug middle-class tradition on which they have been nourished in
the past, acquire a realistic understanding of the forces that actually rule the world, and formulate a fundamental program of
thought and action that will deal honestly and intelligently with
the problems of industrial civilization. They will have to restate
their philosophy of education, reorganize the procedures of the
school, and redefine their own position in society. Such measures
will of course require fundamental changes in the methods of
teacher training and the assumption on the part of the profession
of an increasing burden of cultural leadership.

Our philosophy of education should be securely rooted in the
democratic-revolutionary tradition of the American people, but
should bathe its branches in the atmosphere of industrial civiliza-

tion and the world of nations. It should aim to foster in boys and girls a profound sense of human worth, a genuine devotion to the welfare of the masses, a deep aversion to the tyranny of privilege, a warm feeling of kinship with all the races of mankind, and a quick readiness to engage in bold social experimentation. It should also accept industrial society as an established fact, cease casting nostalgic eyes towards the agrarian past, take up boldly the challenge of the present, recognize the corporate and interdependent character of the contemporary order, and transfer the democratic tradition from individualistic to collectivist economic foundations. It should point toward a productive and distributive system managed in the interests of all who labor, and toward a society marked by comparative equality of material condition and dominated by the ideal of guaranteeing to every child born into the nation the fullest opportunities for personal growth. This would involve the frank abandonment of the doctrines of laissez faire, the administration for the common good of the means of production, and the wide adoption of the principle of social and economic planning.

Such a philosophy clearly calls for a reorganization of the procedures of the school. Yet more imperative, however, is a change in atmosphere, orientation, and outlook. In the collectivist society now emerging the school should be regarded, not as an agency for lifting gifted individuals out of the class into which they were born and of elevating them into favored positions where they may exploit their less fortunate fellows, but rather as an agency for the abolition of all artificial social distinctions and of organizing the energies of the nation for the promotion of the general welfare. This of course does not mean that the individual should not be encouraged to succeed. It means instead that he should be given a new measure of success. In fact the general welfare requires the very highest development of the socially desirable talents of the population. It cannot tolerate the burying of gifts under the accidents of birth or misfortune.

Throughout the school program the development of the social rather than the egoistic impulses should be stressed: and the motive of personal aggrandizement should be subordinated to social ends. In promotion practices, in school activities, in the relations of pupils and teachers and administrators, the ideal of a cooperative commonwealth should prevail, due allowance being made for the requirements of special knowledge and the discharge of social responsibility. Of crucial importance is the position of the teacher in the educational enterprise. Since men and women of feeble personality have no place in the school, however proficient they may be in a particular branch of subject-matter, the entire program for the conduct and administration of education should be directed toward freeing the personality of the teacher for growth in social competence and usefulness. If the system fails here, it fails utterly. All of this applies quite as strictly to the nursery, the kindergarten, and the elementary school as to the secondary school, the college, and the university.

The curriculum should present a two-fold aspect. On the one side, it should provide for the development of the diverse abilities and gifts of the population; on the other, it should represent the highest possible integration of natural resources, cultural heritage, and technology in serving the general good and in fulfilling the democratic ideal. In addition to the mastery of the tools of knowledge and the basic concepts necessary to life in industrial society, the materials of instruction should emphasize the history of human labor, the evolution of peaceful culture, the development of democracy, the rise of industrial civilization, the trend toward collectivism in economy, the emergence of a world order, the conflicts and contradictions in contemporary society, and the various theories, philosophies and plans of action designed to deal with the difficulties and problems of the age. In the sphere of occupational preparation an effort should be made to coordinate the numerous educational facilities and institutions of the nation and to adjust the program of training to the calculated needs of the economy. Also, since the future should see a much further reduction in the hours of labor and a corresponding increase in the hours of leisure, much attention should be given in the curriculum to the development of the recreational interests of the coming generation. The proper utilization of leisure should create a veritable cultural revolution among the masses.

The fact must of course be recognized that the school is by no means an all-powerful educational agency. Ordinarily it touches the child only after he has passed through his six most formative years. Then during the age of schooling its care embraces but one-sixth of his waking hours. Throughout his life, in varying measure and emphasis as the years pass, the individual feels the impact of the family, the community, the church, the playground, innumerable gangs and groups and clubs and societies, and that mighty array of agencies which have either appeared or waxed powerful within recent generations—the railroad, the telegraph, the telephone, the automobile, the airplane, the press, the library, the movie, and the radio. In spite of the fact that the school has developed with great rapidity during the past century, it remains today a relatively feeble instrument with which to refashion society. Yet under bold and competent direction it should be able, as an occasional page of history reveals, to leave a positive imprint on the life of our people. Under really gifted and inspired direction it might even provide a measure of social leadership.

Another point to be stressed, however, is that in capitalistic society the school is greatly weakened by its isolation from life. Although this is due in part to the perpetuation of the tradition of the cloister and the persistence of certain ancient infirmities of the pedagogue, it may be traced largely to that sharp line which divides public from private interest. Whereas sound education requires that the school be intimately linked with community activities, business enterprise demands that the school not trespass upon certain broad fields of life. So long as private gain-seeking is the dominant motif in the social drama, the school will of necessity be forced into an artificial world and formal education will be pushed out upon the periphery of existence. Thus are we brought face to face with the paradox: the school must participate in the task of social reconstruction, yet until society is already transformed the school can scarcely hope to function effectively. The resolution of the paradox is doubtless found in the fact that the process of building a new society will have to go on simultaneously both within and outside the school. Also, whatever the difficulties, the work of the school must be linked in the highest possible degree with the life of the community.

The inadequacy of an educational program that is confined wholly to children must also be frankly recognized. Any program designed for the coming generation, if it is to be successful, must march hand in hand and be closely coordinated with a program of adult and parent education. Particularly is it necessary to reach the young men and women of the nation. To assume that in some unexplained way boys and girls can be emancipated from the control of their elders and be made the sole instruments for building a bet-

ter world is to indulge in the most idle romancing. In the absence
of an enlightened dictatorship, an enlightened form of education
for children is only possible in a community of enlightened men
and women. The progressive wing of the teaching profession therefore should assume responsibility for leadership in acquainting the
adult population, as fully as possible, with the great issues raised
by the onward sweep of industrial civilization. And in this integration of the education of children and adults the chasm separating
school from life would be partially bridged.

In the last analysis the power of organized education rests with
the teacher. Consequently, the most crucial question raised by the
suggestion that the school should boldly enter the world of the living, pertains to the role of the teacher in society. First of all, if the
profession is to be a factor in the process of social reconstruction,
its members must prepare to struggle cooperatively and valiantly
for their rights and ideas. They must fight for tenure, for adequate
compensation, for a voice in the formulation of educational policies; they must uphold the ancient doctrine of academic freedom
and maintain all of their rights as human beings and American citizens. Also they must insist on the public recognition of their professional competence in the field of education: they must oppose
every effort on the part of publishing houses, business interests,
privileged classes, and patriotic societies to prescribe the content
of the curriculum. And in the performance of their own special
functions they should always keep in the closest possible touch
with the great masses of the people, conscious of their struggles
and sensitive to their aspirations. Then to the extent that they succeed in winning a position of genuine leadership in the councils
and the cultural life of the nation, they can expect to attract to
their ranks increasing numbers of young men and women of courage and ability who will always desire to participate in the decision
of great issues. Let them fail in these things, and the appeal to education can only end in disillusionment.

If the teacher is to assume such a role in society, a vastly enriched program of training is imperative. Particularly is this the
case in the preparation of those who are to occupy positions of
leadership and administrative responsibility in the schools. The
analogy between the teacher and the dentist, between the teacher
and the engineer, or even between the teacher and the physician is
totally misleading. Above all, the teacher is a bearer of culture and

a creator of social values. The need therefore is for a training of great breadth and depth. A teachers college, to be worthy of the name, should be a center of truly liberal education. The emphasis on methodology should be secondary; the emphasis on ideas and understanding primary. Education itself should be recognized, not as an independent and universal technique, but as an inseparable aspect of a particular culture in evolution. If education is ever divorced from this broad social process, it becomes formal and sterile. A teachers college in the United States consequently should organize its curriculum about American culture in its world setting—its history, its present status, its future prospects, its basic trends and movements. Only from an institution with such an orientation can come persons qualified to participate actively and intelligently in the life of their time.

The point should also be stressed that the teacher is a citizen. The practical recognition of this fairly obvious truth is a matter of deep significance. The failure of the school to grapple courageously and honestly with the problems of life is unquestionably due in large measure to a like failure on the part of the teacher. If the school is isolated from the great currents that are sweeping through contemporary society, the teacher is no less so. He leads an academic and sheltered life. All too commonly he knows little and cares less about the troubles of the world, except as they may affect immediately his own livelihood. He recoils from contact with reality and even hesitates to fight his own battles. The only remedy for this condition is for the teacher to claim his rights and accept his responsibilities as a citizen and meet his peers from other callings in the arena of political and cultural controversy. Let the profession as a whole pursue such a course, and a further step will be taken toward closing the gap which now separates school from society. The school will then be in a position to exert its maximum influence on the course of events.

The Rights and Responsibilities of Teachers*

The conception of education developed [here] makes heavy demands on the teacher. It requires far more than the following of a

*Education and American Civilization (New York: Teachers College Press, Columbia University, 1952), pp. 451-71.

set of prescribed rules and techniques, the practice of a body of
esoteric knowledge regarding the learning process and the maturation of the young. It even requires of him far more than a mastery
of his specialty and methods of teaching. It requires of him also, as
a frame and guide for all that he does, a deep understanding of our
developing civilization in both its historical and its world setting.
It requires finally that he be sensitive to the profound moral implications of his calling—that he strive to express in his own life and
work, both as teacher and as citizen, a great and noble conception
of the life and destiny of man. All training of teachers, all administrative procedures, all methods of instruction, and all aspects of
the curriculum, if not illuminated and inspired by such a conception, are destined to mediocrity and confusion of purpose, perhaps
to futility and obscurantism.

The task of the teacher is made more difficult by the condition
of cultural transition which marks the current epoch. It is of
course commonplace to speak of the present as a period of swift
social change. Yet the scope and depth of this change, with its implications for education, are insufficiently recognized. The fact is
that the very foundation and framework of our civilization and
social institutions are being profoundly modified. For some time
now, for several generations at least, we have been moving with
growing speed and momentum from the agrarian civilization of the
founding fathers to a new civilization which we are coming to call
industrial. As in all transitional epochs, men are being compelled
to make the great choices. Education must be geared to the task of
assisting our people in the making of these choices. If we are not
to experience a prolonged period of trouble, bordering on catastrophe, education must give understanding of the conditions and
bring clarification to the issues involved. It must play a central role
in building the new minds required by the new age. It must engage
in the perpetual reconstruction of its own methods and purposes.
Although the teacher cannot and should not discharge this responsibility alone, he will have to provide much of the leadership required.

The task of the teacher is made more difficult also by the sweep,
complexity, and dynamism of the American community. The surface of this community is always agitated, while in times of national crisis storms of political passion may penetrate its lowest
depths. Local and nationwide organized interests, as we have seen,

struggle incessantly to achieve their diverse and conflicting purposes. Powerful groups play upon the school, each striving to impose its will on the substance and processes of education. To surrender to these pressures would rob the school of its integrity and convert it into a kind of weather vane which would show the direction of the wind at the moment but would scarcely bring the ship of education to any port, except by chance. Some perhaps would seek tranquility by having the school retire from the world, renounce all controversial matters, and devote itself to the teaching of the "fundamentals" and the "training of the mind." Unfortunately for this proposal an educational program cannot be launched without confronting and making decisions regarding the most fundamental issues of value and purpose. And modern psychology has demonstrated that the training of the mind does not take place in a social and cultural vacuum. This can only mean, at least in a free society, that the teacher must be more than a tool or a "weapon," to use Stalin's term, of political power.

The task of the teacher is made yet more difficult by the presence in the American community of many other agencies and influences which mold mind and character. While the school is the one institution that is wholly dedicated by society to the work of education, it is by no means entirely responsible for the rearing of the young, even though irate citizens often charge it with failure to eradicate ignorance, stupidity, delinquency, corruption, and other ills common to humanity. The fact is that the school has supervision over children and youth from birth to eighteen years of age during only about one-eighth to one-seventh of their waking hours, if they are in attendance every day the school is in session. During the remaining hours they are subjected to the influences of family, neighborhood, and church, street, gang, sport, camp, and industry. And in these days of advanced technology we must add the powerful agencies of mass communication—the comic, the movie, the radio, and the video whose controlling purposes are not education, but profit, entertainment, and perhaps propaganda. With all of these forces competing with and often ranged against the school, it is astonishing that the teacher is able to accomplish as much as he does in the civilizing of the young. Yet this challenge must be confronted, and it can be confronted successfully only by making the work of the school so vital that its influence will pervade in some measure the entire life of children and youth.

The teacher is inadequately equipped to discharge the duties of his profession in the present age. Although great advances have been made during the past two generations, the teacher is the victim of a severe cultural lag. While the demands made upon the school by the changed conditions of life have greatly increased, the popular conception of the calling remains rooted largely in the preindustrial epoch.

The difficulty may be traced in part to the origins of our system of common schools. That system was not imposed from above by a strong central government or an influential intellectual class. Rather were its foundations laid by relatively untutored farmers who established one-room district schools in rural neighborhoods as they moved across the continent. In their eyes the school was a minor social and educational institution. Its work was encompassed by "book larnin," and "book larnin" was a simple matter of reading, writing, and arithmetic. They could therefore see little reason for an elaborate program of teacher training. To them it seemed entirely appropriate to ask a bright boy or girl graduate of the eighth grade to return to school and teach the things he or she had just learned. Thus there developed in the United States the tradition of the professionally untrained teacher. In a later generation many of our people viewed with scorn and ridicule the proposal that farm boys and girls should study agriculture and housekeeping.

Under these conditions teaching was not taken too seriously. It ranked low among the occupations as a life career. It was poorly paid, marked by insecurity of tenure, and hedged about by all sorts of petty restrictions and annoyances. It was regarded as a task suited to the undeveloped powers of youth approaching manhood and womanhood, as a steppingstone to marriage or some adult calling or profession. As late as the middle of the nineteenth century many teachers in the most progressive states were under twenty-one years of age and the great majority departed the school after one, two, three, four, or five years of teaching. Those who remained longer were often looked upon as a "little queer," as human culls who could not "make the grade" in the rough and tumble of life, as women who failed to find husbands or as men who feared to compete with their peers in the economic struggle.[1]

This conception of the teacher was given satirical expression by
Washington Irving in the character of Ichabod Crane. Many an
American citizen doubtless has greeted with a chuckle of approval
the observation of Henry L. Mencken: "The average schoolmaster
. . . is and always must be essentially an ass, for how can one imagine an intelligent man engaging in so puerile an avocation?[2] And
how often have we heard a banker, a physician, or even a teacher
evoke condescending laughter with George Bernard Shaw's famous
gibe, "He who can, does: he who cannot, teaches!" But how many
know that the great dramatist also said, "He who can do, does: he
who can think, teachers"?[3]

. . . .

From earliest historical times the word teacher has generally carried a lofty connotation. The great prophets of mankind have been
called teachers. According to an old Chinese saying, which reflects
the high regard for learning of this enduring civilization, "a great
teacher is like a spring breeze and seasonal rain." Cicero inquired:
"What greater or better gift can we offer the republic than to teach
and instruct our youth?" Franklin, Washington, Jefferson, and
others among our founding fathers regarded teaching as a noble
profession. And throughout our history men and women of highest idealism and talents have given themselves unsparingly to the
cause of education. Moreover, the improvement of the preparation
and the raising of the status of the teacher have advanced notably
during the last several generations. Today, in terms of social idealism and devotion to the general welfare, teachers as a group are
unsurpassed by any other comparable body of citizens. Yet, as we
shall see later, much remains to be done. The old heritage lingers
on. In 1947-48 many teachers in the American common schools
had received no college training whatsoever, and less than 15 percent held the master's or a higher degree.[4] Moreover, in five states
more than 40 percent of the teachers received less than fifteen
hundred dollars a year.[5] Clearly the task of building a profession
capable of discharging the heavy responsibilities of public education in the present epoch is only well begun. Our American conception of the teacher still lags far behind our expressed convictions regarding the worth and power of education.

As a people we are inadequately prepared to support the teacher in the discharge of his essential functions in a free society. That
we are far from ready to provide the financial and material re-

sources necessary to the fulfillment of our democratic faith and professions in the field of education need not be elaborated here. It is well known that the common rate of compensation is quite insufficient by itself to attract the more talented of our youth, to justify the long period of arduous training required, and to enable the teacher to live a rich and full life. It has often been remarked that we seem to be more interested in the condition of our school buildings than in the excellence of our teachers.

The most conspicuous failure of our people, however, is found in the realm of understanding. We lack a clear and comprehensive understanding of the nature of education in a free society. Boards of education seem to regard the teacher as something less than a first-class citizen or a complete person. They are inclined to frown upon teachers accepting fees for speeches, living in apartments if unmarried, failing to attend church, playing pool or billiards, going to public dances, or joining a teachers' union. They are very much opposed to teachers smoking in public, playing cards just for fun, teaching controversial issues, making a political speech, or running for political office. Also they are decidedly of the opinion that a woman should not teach after marriage.[6] That the teacher should be expected to live by higher moral standards than the ordinary citizen is readily granted. The fact that an individual is able to keep out of jail scarcely qualifies him for the high calling of supervising the rearing of the young. Yet there is undoubtedly much in the treatment of the teacher that not only consigns him to an inferior status in the community, but also impairs his qualities as a guardian of the tradition of human freedom. It would seem, moreover, that boards of education sometimes think that he should be compelled to live in an earlier generation, if not in the agrarian age itself.

The teacher is the natural prey of busybodies and pressure groups, partly perhaps because of his weakness. Without shame they often act as if the school belonged to them and the teachers were their liveried servants. They strive to throw out textbooks, to determine methods of instruction, to force their special interests into the curriculum, and to secure the discharge of qualified teachers of independent mind. Individuals and organizations professing the highest purposes seek to influence through political pressures and propaganda campaigns the program and personnel of the school. Sometimes bigots and ignoramuses gather people of like qualities around themselves and launch wholly vicious and irresponsible attacks on members of the profession in the name of the preservation of American liberties. That such assaults upon the teacher rarely arouse the wrath of the general body of citizens is evidence of political and intellectual immaturity in the realm of the conduct of public education.

There is of course a problem here. It is not suggested that a "law be passed" to protect the school. The cure would certainly be worse than the disease. Moreover, the informed interest of citizens in the schools in both their individual and their organized capacities is to be desired and encouraged. Such interest is indispensable in order to keep education in touch with changing conditions of life. And toleration of the "lunatic fringe" is doubtless a part of the price which men must pay for a free society. Yet much of present practice reflects a lack of understanding on the part of both teachers and citizens of the nature and function of education in our democracy.

The training of the teacher must be greatly broadened and deepened. The central theme [here] is that education always expresses some conception of civilization and that, regardless of the efficiency of its procedures, it can rise no higher than the conception of civilization which determines its substance and purpose. Since the teacher must ever be the living embodiment of this conception, it follows that the education of a society can rise no higher than the qualifications, physical, intellectual, aesthetic, and moral, of its teachers. The conception of civilization developed in these pages obviously requires profound changes in the program of professional preparation.

First of all we must abandon or enrich much that is in our heritage. We must abandon completely the idea that teaching at any level is a simple process whose elements can be mastered in a few months or even several years by bright boys and girls in the period of late adolescence. We must abandon completely the tradition derived from our simple agrarian past that teaching is a matter of keeping order and transmitting verbal skills to embellish the genuine education acquired in the home and on the farm. We must abandon also the tradition derived from the class societies of the Old World that teaching in the common school involves merely giving to the offspring of the "hewers of wood and drawers of water" the narrow training required by that humble station in the social order to which they are called by the laws of God and man. We must abandon too the idea derived from the early period of industrialization that teaching has as its main object the preparation of ambitious youth to "get ahead" of their fellows in the race for preferred positions in the economic and social order. We must abandon likewise the assumption that teaching is essentially a process of passing on to the young various bodies of knowledge and that the level of teaching bears a direct relation to the abstruseness of the knowledge involved. We must abandon finally the idea derived from business management that the teacher is merely a semi-skilled worker in the assembly line who is expected to follow without question the orders of his immediate superior in a mass-production enterprise.

We must see teaching as the tremendous and difficult task that it is. We must see that it involves nothing less than the guiding of the individual to full maturity and freedom, of inducting him into the most complex and dynamic society of history, of preparing him to assume the heavy duties of managing that society and of transmitting its heritage of liberty unimpaired and even enhanced to his children. The assumption of the post of teaching at any level of the school system is indeed a sobering and challenging responsibility, and hardly to be assigned to the ill-prepared or the ill-disposed. Who can say that the task is easier in the kindergarten than in the university, in the guiding of the total personality of the child than in the teaching of the higher mathematics? About this we need not quarrel. We know that either requires not only professional skill and knowledge of the first order, but also charity, understanding, and wisdom.

Since the days of Samuel R. Hall and James G. Carter, who toward the close of the first quarter of the nineteenth century founded the first institutions to prepare young people for "school keeping," the need for the professional training of the teacher has been increasingly recognized in America. With the unparalleled expansion of the common school during subsequent generations, and particularly since the opening of the present century, the program for the training of teachers has been greatly extended. Today the need for such a program is generally accepted. Yet the actual practice lags far behind the evolution of American civilization and the conception of education. The professional training of the teacher continues to bear the stamp of its humble origins in the agrarian age. It is severely limited in both scope and content. In terms of depth and breadth of preparation teaching remains today a skilled or at best a semiprofessional occupation. The emphasis is still on the mechanics of education, on methods of teaching, on "school keeping," on mastery of narrow subject matter, on financial and material operations. All of these things are of course necessary, but they are scarcely sufficient to equip even the most gifted to discharge the obligations of rearing the young in the atomic age. The time has come for us to consign to the wastebasket of history the idea that teaching requires less severe selection and training than the practice of medicine, law, engineering, or theology. Indeed, from the standpoint of the values and responsibilities involved teaching is probably the most difficult and important of all the professions.

In addition to the mastery of techniques and specialized subject matter, every teacher should be expected to acquire a basic understanding of the nature of the child and of man. This would of course mean knowledge of the biological constitution of the species, of the role of hereditary forces, of the laws of growth, learning, and maturation, of the development of character and personality, of the whole process of the induction of the young into the life of the group. It would mean also the acquisition of those insights and perspectives which can come only from some acquaintance with man in the natural order, in history, and in diverse cultures. The value of knowledge of psychology has of course long been recognized, and with the revolutionary advances in the science during the past two generations it has thoroughly established itself in the program. However, even today the emphasis is placed too largely on the relation of the individual to the learning of "subject matter." The educational psychology of the future must be increasingly social in character. It must devote far more attention than heretofore to the relation of the individual to the group and the entire field of human relations. The complexity and dynamism of industrial society, as well as the moral commitments of democracy, make this shift in emphasis clearly necessary.

At this point we come to the central and crucial deficiency in our program of teacher training—a deficiency which is derived from the limitations of our traditional conception of education. According to that conception education should and can be conducted in conformity with the universal laws of the organism and

its own nature. Adequate understanding of the process can therefore be gained through the study of the child and the school. The
thesis [presented here] on the other hand, is that the whole enterprise of education is a function of a particular society at a particular time and place and must express some conception of life and
civilization supported by the social group involved. This view vastly complicates the task of the teacher in a free society and, if con-
sistently applied, would call for nothing less than a revolution in
the program of professional training.

If the education of the young involves in some measure not only
the fortunes of individuals, but also the future of our society and
civilization, of our democratic institutions and free way of life, as
it clearly does, then the selection and preparation of teachers
should be recognized by all as a major concern of the Republic,
certainly as important as the production of material things or
even the maintenance of the national defense. Indeed, if conceived
in appropriate terms and with adequate vision, it is the most basic
and decisive factor in survival and progress. Johann Valentin Andreae, seventeenth-century humanist, long ago gave voice to an
ideal which free society should always cherish. "Their instructors,"
he said of teachers in his mythical community of Christianopolis,
"are not men from the dregs of human society nor such as are use-
less for other occupations, but the choice of all the citizens, persons whose standing in the republic is known and who very often
have access to the highest positions in the state."[7] In these words
Andreae was merely saying that our children, all of our children,
constitute our most precious resource.

For a teacher to be ignorant of the history of his people, of
their triumphs and failures, of their basic ways and institutions, of
their points of weakness and strength, of their moral commitments
and ideals, of the great patterns of their civilization, of the dangers
which threaten them, and of the opportunities which confront
them is to invite catastrophe in the present age. Yet it must be con-
ceded that our program of teacher training today must plead guilty
in considerable measure to this indictment. The fact is that few
American teachers are able to outline except in most superficial
terms the basic features of our civilization or our way of life. Fewer still have reasoned and informed convictions regarding the foundations of free society and the forces at home and abroad which
place in jeopardy our entire heritage of human liberty. And yet

fewer have more than a most superficial knowledge of the great ethical, aesthetic, philosophical, and religious traditions of Western man on which our entire civilization rests. The explanation of this situation undoubtedly must be attributed largely to deficiencies in their training. They are simply not expected to be interested in or to probe deeply into such questions.

Whatever may be said about other forms of professional preparation a teacher-training institution should make central the study of our American civilization in both its historical and its world setting, from its origins in antiquity to its relations with all nations and peoples. Whether the individual is to practice his calling in the kindergarten or the university, in the teaching of literature or science, he should know both the society and the culture which the school is supposed to serve. To aspire to less than this in the contemporary world is certain to provide an education of inferior quality and possibly to court catastrophe. Clearly, if teachers are to assist effectively in the rearing of a generation of free men, they must themselves have the knowledge and the loyalties necessary to set and keep men free.

. . . .

The life of the teacher must be greatly enriched. First of all the teacher must be relieved from excessive demands on his time and energies. He must be assured those working conditions which are essential to the successful discharge of his heavy responsibilities. This means the reduction of class size and teaching load to the point that makes it possible for him to know his pupils individually, to become acquainted with their parents and home surroundings, and to participate effectively in the formulation of school policy and the development of the curriculum. It means also the complete abandonment of the tradition that the teacher is merely a more or less high-grade servant who may be called upon at will by members of the board of education or private persons of power and influence in the community to perform manifold duties ranging from the teaching of Sunday school to the administration of an essay contest on the virtues of advertising. Only when an individual feels that he is doing his job well can he experience that sense of personal dignity and satisfaction in his calling which is the highest reward of socially useful and creative labor. It is only then, too, that the community is likely to appreciate fully the work of the teacher.

In the second place, the teacher must be free to participate as a mature person in the life of the community—local, state, and national. Indeed, such participation should be encouraged and rewarded. This calls for the abandonment of the tradition that the teacher should be something less than a whole human being, that he should lead a cloistered existence, that he should always remain as immature as the boys and girls who wielded the "hickory stick" and taught "readin', 'ritin', and 'rithmetic" in the one-room district school of hallowed memory. Teachers today, whether men or women, should be expected to engage in courtship, to marry, and to have children of their own. They should be expected to join and aspire to leadership in organizations devoted to the promotion of the general welfare, the advancement of the arts and sciences of life, or the simple enjoyment of good fellowship. They should be expected to pursue avocational interests of the greatest variety, from hiking to music and from stamp collecting to horticulture. Through appropriate conditions of work and adequate remuneration they should be assured leisure and funds necessary for travel, purchase of books, attendance at the theater, and general cultivation of personal interests. Perhaps even more than other citizens they should set an example to the young by taking an active part in civic affairs and exercising responsibly all the rights of citizenship. They should join political parties, make political speeches, and run for public office. There is of course no suggestion here that every teacher should do all of these things. Like others of his generation he should be allowed freedom of choice. The point to be emphasized is merely that by living a full and rich life he will be a better teacher. No one can truly understand our American community by reading books and following the role of a spectator.

In the third place, teachers should be as free to form their own organizations as any other group of citizens. This right is implied in the foregoing paragraph. But the issue is so important that it merits special consideration. It is of course well known that teachers today have many organizations. They are organized at all levels and in all specialties, and they have several organizations which aspire to embrace and represent the profession as a whole. Yet the fact remains that as yet they are not effectively organized to present their case as a whole to the American community.

The object of an adequate organization, aside from the improvement of the processes and purposes of education, should be three-

fold. It should strive to remove the many disabilities and frustra-
tions under which the teacher labors and to which attention has
already been directed. In a world marked by organized pressures,
no group is likely to be heard or even respected if it lacks the resources which come from association. Also the organization should
battle for the common school, for the welfare of the younger generation, and for a conception of education appropriate to the present age. Being closer to these interests than any other group of
citizens, teachers naturally have a special obligation here to the
whole community. Finally, through their organization they should
endeavor to express with power their special point of view with
respect to all the great issues confronting the American people. In
their varied struggles teachers will inevitably work with other
groups which share their values and purposes. Whether they should
affiliate organically with any one element in the population, such
as organized labor, is a highly complicated question whose merits
will not be discussed in these pages. The point to be emphasized
here is that teachers need a powerful organization and that they
will find themselves closely associated with those groups which are
devoted to the cause of public education and democracy.

The American people must achieve a more comprehensive and
profound understanding of the nature of education in a free society. Throughout our history as a nation we have had great faith in
the school and have assumed that in some way it is a dependable
guardian of democracy. Yet, with the exception of small minorities
in the population, we have never been fully aware of the fact that
a free society requires a very special kind of education. Since civil
and political liberty is one of the basic values of our civilization
and since it is under great threat in the world today, these conclud-
ing paragraphs will be devoted to a consideration of certain aspects
of this issue.

In a democracy the people rule themselves, either directly or in-
directly. In a democracy power rests ultimately in the hands of the
citizens. Under appropriate constitutional guarantees and provi-
sions they control the state and may alter it in accordance with
their wishes. In a democracy political liberty and the process of
revolution itself are institutionalized. It is assumed that the most
fundamental changes in the social order can be achieved peaceful-
ly through education and enlightenment. In such a society, therefore, the exercise of control over the schools by the state would

appear to constitute something of a contradiction or at least a
hazard. Potentially there is always the danger that the political authority may seek to convert the entire educational process into an
instrument dedicated to the rearing of a generation of subjects or
slaves. In the present industrial age, with the trend on the one side
toward the concentration of power in the hands of government
and the trend on the other toward the expansion of the institutions of organized education, the threat to the perdurance of a
society of free men is evident. The totalitarian pattern for the
molding of the mind might make its way unobtrusively in the
most democratic state. The American Federation of Labor, peer-
less champion of public education and ardent defender of free institutions, by convention action in 1950 formulated in these
words the principle which should guide us: "Enlightened citizens
of free nations should, through their thinking, control their government; but a democratic government should never attempt, through
legislation, to control the thinking of its citizens." The traditional
fear on the part of the American people of federal control of education is not without significance here. The same may be said of
their invention of the independent board of education.

The resolution of this contradiction or difficulty, however, requires much more than institutional safeguards. It requires the development of powerful supporting traditions. And this requires the
acquisition by the people of a clear conception of the nature of
democratic education. . . . Such an education is not necessarily one
which the people at a given time may want, even though they do
constitute the final authority. The current epoch has amply
demonstrated the truth of the proposition that in a moment of
crisis or passion they may approve unwittingly measures which
will destroy their liberties and reduce them to bondage. The old
adage that "the voice of the people is the voice of God" is true
only with reservations. Unsustained by reasoned loyalties and un-
informed by relevant knowledge, the people may respond to the
violent shouts of the demagogue and open the gates to despotism.
A truly democratic education is one that is designed to guard and
strengthen the free way of life through the generations. We in
America lack a clear grasp of the nature of the educational problem in this relationship.

If education is to serve the ends of democracy during the
troubled years ahead, the American people will have to achieve

the necessary understanding. First of all, democratic education is committed to the basic values and processes of democracy, to the conception of human equality, dignity, and worth, to all the civil and political liberties. It must therefore be designed to bring the individual to full maturity as a free person, to foster enlightenment and release creative energies and talents. It must be earnestly committed to the transmission, cultivation, and enrichment of the great tradition of intellectual inquiry and artistic expression. A democratic education must be sensitive and responsive to the changing foundations, the deep-flowing currents, and the emerging conditions and potentialities of industrial society in both its domestic and world relations. At the same time it must be removed in some measure from the passions and narrowly partisan struggles of the moment. Amid the present confusion of tongues and conflict of ideologies the school should be a stabilizing force, a place of calm and serenity, a center for the nurture of the intellectual virtues. It should be a place where the honest questions of the young may be raised with the assurance that they will receive honest consideration. We must always remember that the school is a temple erected to the future, a shrine dedicated to the *long* future of our society and mankind.

An education so conceived is not to be attained by responding to every wind that blows, nor by remaking itself after every election. On the contrary, while it can never be autonomous, it should enjoy a large measure of independence from the pressures of private persons, minorities, classes, organizations, parties, churches, and even government officials. The establishment of this condition of freedom and independence for the school should be a major responsibility of the state in a democratic society. This means that members of boards of education must not only protect the school from external demands but also voluntarily restrain themselves in the exercise of power. The desired condition, moreover, cannot be achieved by the passing of laws, but only by the development of an appropriate tradition shared alike by both citizen and teacher.

The Teacher in a Free Society*

The role here assigned to organized education in the rising battle for democracy in America requires a teacher of large intellectual and moral stature—a teacher who is more than a technician, more than a skillful practitioner of the art of pedagogy. He should indeed be a thorough master of his craft; but he should also know to what larger ends his craftsmanship is directed. He should be a scholar who has command of the knowledge of his specialty, a citizen who takes a responsible part in the life of the community, a democrat who identifies himself with the interests and fortunes of the many, a patriot who is deeply concerned over the future of his country and his people, a friend of mankind who cherishes the values of world peace and human brotherhood, a poet who feels the tragedy, the pathos, the glorious hopes of the time, a wise counselor of the young who knows the conditions and problems of living in the present confused and challenging epoch. He should also be an active member of his profession, ready to devote time and energy to the general advancement of the cause of public education and enlightenment.

This is not to say that the schools and colleges of the country have not had teachers of this type. They have had many of them, but they need many more. The number may be increased perhaps by providing a more generous program of preparation—a program that will go beyond the techniques of the classroom and place large emphasis on the social, cultural, and philosophical foundations of education—a program systematically designed to develop a person of liberal and humane outlook. But more important than the mode of training are the conditions under which the teacher lives and works. Anything that enlarges the opportunities and responsibilities of the calling will inevitably enlarge the intellectual and moral stature of the individual teacher. For such opportunities and responsibilities the members of the profession should struggle without ceasing. And in this struggle they should have the support of all citizens who would have the schools serve the cause of American democracy more effectively.

*The Prospects of American Democracy (New York: John Day Co., 1938), pp. 346-47.

Notes

1. The Professional Life

1. George S. Counts, "A Humble Autobiography," in *Leaders in Education*, ed. Robert J. Havighurst. Seventieth Yearbook of the National Society for the Study of Education, vol. 70, pt. 2 (Chicago: N.S.S.E., 1971), p. 158.

2. "Charles H. Judd," *Leaders in Education*, 2d ed. (New York: Science Press, 1941), p. 543.

3. Ida B. De Pencier, *The History of the Laboratory Schools, the University of Chicago 1896-1965* (Chicago: Quadrangle Books, 1967), pp. 71-72.

4. *The Department of Education at Yale University, 1891-1958* (New Haven: Yale University, 1960), p. 16.

5. *New York Times*, 20 May 1929, p. 24.

6. Counts, "A Humble Autobiography," pp. 159-60.

7. Beard to Counts, 7 February [1933], Special Collections, Southern Illinois University at Carbondale.

8. Ibid.

9. George S. Counts, *Alumnus* (Carbondale: Southern Illinois University, March 1969), p. 10.

10. *New York Times Book Review*, 27 July 1930, p. 1.

11. Jesse H. Newlon to A. C. Krey, 27 July 1931, Joseph Regenstein Library, University of Chicago.

12. American Historical Association, *Conclusions and Recommendations of the Commission* (New York: Charles Scribner's Sons, 1934), p. vii.

13. Counts to Judd, 30 October 1929, Joseph Regenstein Library, University of Chicago.

14. Beard to Counts, 5 August [1934], Special Collections, Southern Illinois University at Carbondale.

15. Howard Whitman, "Progressive Education—Which Way Forward?" *Colliers* 123 (14 May 1954), p. 25.

16. Counts to Beard, 16 February 1934, Special Collections, Southern Illinois University at Carbondale.

17. *New York Times*, 17 September 1934, p. 19.

18. William Edward Eaton, *The American Federation of Teachers, 1916-1961* (Carbondale: Southern Illinois University Press, 1975), pp. 111-21.

19. *Time*, 20 July 1936, p. 68.

20. *New York Times*, 7 November 1941, p. 16.

21. *New York Times*, 23 August 1942, p. 37.

22. *New York Times*, 6 September 1952, p. 9.

23. *New York Times*, 5 November 1952, p. 1.

24. Application by George S. Counts, 15 May 1962, Southern Illinois University.

25. Theodore Sizer, *Places for Learning, Places for Joy* (Cambridge: Harvard University Press, 1973), pp. 32-33.

26. [George S. Counts], *A Call to the Teachers of the Nation* (New York: John Day Co., 1933), p. 23.

27. Childs to Counts, 26 April 1971, Special Collections, Southern Illinois University at Carbondale.

28. Counts, "A Humble Autobiography," p. 155.

2. American History and National Character

1. Michael Chevalier, *Society, Manners and Politics in the United States* (Boston: Weeks, Jordan and Co., 1839), p. 285.

2. Ibid., p. 286.

3. *New York Times*, 9 November 1930, p. 12.

4. Alexis de Tocqueville, *Democracy in America* (New York: The Century Co., 1898), 2:213-14.

5. Ibid., p. 213.

6. John Bradbury, "Travels in the Interior of America, in the Years 1809, 1810, and 1811," in *Early Western Travels*, ed. Reuben Gold Thwaites (Cleveland: Arthur H. Clark Co., 1904), 5:282-83.

7. John Woods, "Two Years' Residence in the Settlement of the English Prairie, in the Illinois Country, United States," in *Early Western Travels*, 10:300.

8. James B. Ireland was born in Kentucky in 1797 and lived through the nineteenth century in his native state, following the occupation of farming. In connection with the celebration of the 100th anniversary of his birth in 1897 he set down his recollections under the title *Looking Backward Through 100 Years*. The manuscript was published in the Hancock Clarion, Harnsville, Hancock County, Kentucky, in 1898.

9. *New York Times*, 23 January 1938, sec. 4, p. 9.

10. George Gallup, "The American Mind: A Test of Democracy," *New York Times Magazine*, 24 April 1938, pp. 1-2.

11. "Press vs. Public," *New Republic*, 90 (March 17, 1937), 178.

3. Education and Social Forces

1. Merle Curti, *The Social Ideas of American Educators* (New York: Charles Scribner's Sons, 1935), p. 334.

4. Technology and Industrialism

1. Leo Hausleiter, *The Machine Unchained* (New York: D. Appleton-Century Co., 1933), p. 12.

2. National Resources Committee, *Technological Trends and National Policy* (Washington, 1937), p. 263.

3. U.S. Department of Labor, Bureau of Labor Statistics, *50 Years Progress of American Labor* (Washington, 1950), p. 8.

4. J. D. Bernal, "Science and Industry," in *The Frustration of Science*, by Daniel Hall et al. (New York: W. W. Norton, 1935), p. 54.

5. James T. Shotwell, *War as an Instrument of National Policy* (New York: Harcourt, Brace, and Co., 1929), p. 8.

6. Enid Charles, "The Invention of Sterility," in Hall, p. 104.

5. Totalitarianism and Democracy

1. A. G. Keller, "The Discoverer of the Forgotten Man," *American Mercury* 27 (November 1932), 257.

2. J. B. Bury, *A History of Freedom of Thought* (New York: Henry Holt and Co., 1913), pp. 247-48.

3. C. E. M. Joad, *Liberty To-day* (New York: E. P. Dutton, 1935), p. 3.

4. Wilhelm Stuckart, *Geschichte im Geschichtsunterricht* (Frankfurt am Main: Moritz Diesterweg, 1934), pp. 31-32.

5. Benito Mussolini, "Fascismo," *Enciclopedia Italiana*, 14 (Milan: 1932), 851.

6. Henry Noel Brailsford, *Property or Peace* (New York: Covici, Friede, 1934), p. 43.

7. In the remainder of the argument I confine attention entirely to the domestic situation. I do this, not because I regard the question of international relations unimportant, but rather because of limitations of space. All I can say here is that any proper conception of the world society must accept the principle of the moral equality of races and nations.

6. The American Teacher

1. See Willard S. Elsbree, *The American Teacher* (New York: American Book Co., 1939), pp. 271-305.

2. H. L. Mencken, *Prejudices*, 3d ser. (New York: Alfred A. Knopf, 1922), p. 244.

3. *The W. E. A. Education Year Book* (London: Workers' Educational Association, 1918), pp. 20-21.

4. The Council of State Governments, *The Forty-Eight State School Systems* (Chicago, 1949), p. 70.

5. Ibid., p. 209.

6. See Lloyd Allen Cook and Elaine Forsyth Cook, *A Sociological Approach to Education*, 2d ed. (New York: McGraw-Hill, 1950), p. 447. See

also Howard K. Beale, *Are American Teachers Free?* (New York: Charles Scribner's Sons, 1936).

7. Johann Valentin Andreae, *Christianopolis*, trans. Felix Emil Held (New York: Oxford University Press, 1916), p. 207.

Checklist of the Writings
of George S. Counts

1915

Counts, George S. "Approved High Schools of the North Central Association of Colleges and Secondary Schools." In *A Study of the Colleges and High Schools in the North Central Association*, pp. 31-129. Washington, DC: U.S. Bureau of Education, 1915.

1917

_____. *Arithmetic Tests and Studies in the Psychology of Arithmetic.* Chicago: University of Chicago Press, 1917. 127 pp.

1922

_____. "Education as an Individual Right." *School and Society* 15 (22 April 1922):433-37. ·

_____. "Education for Vocational Efficiency." *School Review* 30 (September 1922):493-513.

_____. "Population of the Private Secondary School." *School and Society* 15 (27 May 1922):569-73.

_____. *The Selective Character of American Secondary Education.* Chicago: University of Chicago Press, 1922. 162 pp.

_____. "The Selective Principle in American Secondary Education." *School Review* 29 (November 1921):657-67; 30 (February 1922): 95-109.

_____. "Social Purpose of the Education of the Gifted Child." *Educational Review* 64 (October 1922):233-44.

1923

_____. "The Social Composition of the High School." *New Republic* 36 (7 November 1923):5-7.

1924

_____. "The Future of the Comprehensive High School." *NEA Proceedings* 62 (1924):796-802.
_____, and Chapman, James C. *Principles of Education.* Boston: Houghton-Mifflin Co., 1924. 645 pp.

1925

_____. "Education in the Philippines." *Elementary School Journal* 26 (October 1925):94-106.
_____. "The Social Status of Occupations: A Problem in Vocational Guidance." *School Review* 33 (January 1925):16-27.

1926

_____, and Rugg, Harold. "A Critical Appraisal of Current Methods of Curriculum-Making." In *The Foundations and Technique of Curriculum-Construction,* pt. 1, pp. 425-47. Prepared under the direction of Harold Rugg. Twenty-Sixth Yearbook of the National Society for the Study of Education. Bloomington, IL: Public School Publishing Co., 1926.
_____. "Current Practices in Curriculum-Making in Public High Schools." In *The Foundations and Technique of Curriculum-Construction,* pt. 1, pp. 135-62. Prepared under the direction of Harold Rugg. Twenty-Sixth Yearbook of the National Society for the Study of Education. Bloomington, IL: Public School for Publishing Co., 1926.
_____. "The Place of the School in the Social Order." *NEA Proceedings* 64 (1926):308-15.
_____. "Procedures in Evaluating Extra-Curriculum Activities." *School Review* 34 (June 1926):412-21.
_____. *The Senior High School Curriculum.* Chicago: University of Chicago Press, 1926. 160 pp.
_____. "Some Notes on the Foundations of Curriculum-Making." In *The Foundations and Technique of Curriculum-Construction,* pt. 2, pp. 73-90. Prepared under the direction of Harold Rugg. Twenty-Sixth Yearbook of the National Society for the Study of Education. Bloomington, IL: Public School Publishing Co., 1926.

1927

_____. *The Social Composition of Boards of Education: A Study in the Social Control of Public Education.* Chicago: University of Chicago Press, 1927. 100 pp.

_____. "Who Shall Make the Curriculum?" *School Review* 35 (May 1927): 332-39.

1928

_____. "The Changing High School Curriculum." *Progressive Education* 5 (October-November-December 1928):335-40.

_____. "Education." *American Journal of Sociology* 34 (July 1928):177-86.

_____. "Education in Soviet Russia." In *Soviet Russia in the Second Decade*, pp. 268-303. Edited by Stuart Chase, Robert Dunn, and Rexford Tugwell. New York: John Day Co., 1928.

_____. "The Educational Program of Soviet Russia." *Bulletin of the National Association of Secondary-School Principals* (March 1928):1-14.

_____. "The Educational Program of Soviet Russia." *NEA Proceedings* 66 (1928):593-602.

_____. *School and Society in Chicago.* New York: Harcourt, Brace, and Co., 1928. 367 pp.

1929

_____. "Criteria for Judging a Philosophy of Education." *School and Society* 30 (27 July 1929):103-7.

_____. [Excerpt] *Research Bulletin of the National Education Society* 7 (September 1929):217.

_____, ed. Translated by Nucia Perlmutter. *The New Education in the Soviet Republic.* By Albert Petrovich Pinkevich. New York: John Day Co., 1929. 403 pp.

_____. *Secondary Education and Industrialism.* Cambridge: Harvard University Press, 1929. 70 pp.

_____. "Selection as a Function of American Secondary Education." *Bulletin of the Department of Secondary-School Principals* (March 1929):82-92.

_____. "Selection as a Function of American Secondary Education." *NEA Proceedings* 67 (1929):596-603.

_____. "What is a School of Education?" *Teachers College Record* 30 (April 1929):647-55.

1930

_____. *The American Road to Culture: A Social Interpretation of Educa-*

tion in the United States. New York: John Day Co., 1930. 194 pp.

_____. "Education and the Five-Year Plan of Soviet Russia." *Journal of Educational Sociology* 4 (September 1930):20-29.

_____. "Education and the Five-Year Plan of Soviet Russia." *NEA Proceedings* 68 (1930):213-18.

_____. *A Ford Crosses Russia.* Boston: The Stratford Co., 1930. 223 pp.

1931

_____, et al. "The Economic Outlook for Russia." *Consensus* 15 (May 1931):13-21.

_____. "Education and the Five-Year Plan of Soviet Russia." In *Education and Economics*, pp. 39-46. Edited by Harold Florian Clark. New York: Teachers College, Columbia University, 1931.

_____. "Education and Social Planning in Soviet Russia." *Proceedings of the Association of History Teachers of the Middle States and Maryland* 29 (1931):32-36.

_____. "Education—History" in *Encyclopaedia of the Social Sciences*, vol. 5. New York: Macmillan Co., pp. 403-14.

_____. "The Great Experiment." *New York Times*, 16 August 1931, sec. 9, p. 2.

_____. Lodge, Nucia P., trans. *New Russia's Primer: The Story of the Five-Year Plan.* By M. Ilin [pseu. I. A. Marshak]. "A Word to the American Reader," by George S. Counts, pp. v-x. Boston and New York: Houghton-Mifflin Co., 1931. 162 pp.

_____. "Russians Educate Through Activities." *New York Times*, 19 July 1931, sec. 3, p. E7.

_____. *The Soviet Challenge to America.* New York: John Day Co., 1931. 372 pp.

1932

_____. "Counts Censures Bennett, Dewey." *New York Times*, 23 August 1932, p. 37.

_____. "Culture and Educational Theory." *Teachers College Record* 33 (April 1932):585-87.

_____. "Dare Progressive Education Be Progressive?" *Progressive Education* 9 (April 1932):257-63.

_____. *Dare the School Build a New Social Order?* New York: John Day Co., 1932. 56pp.

_____. "Education and Indoctrination." Letter to *New Republic* 72 (21 August 1932):75.

_____. "Education—For What? I: The Ten Fallacies of the Educators." *New Republic* 71 (18 May 1932):12-16.

_____. "Education—For What? II: Indoctrination and a Workable Democracy." *New Republic* 71 (25 May 1932):38-41.

_____. "Education Through Indoctrination." *Official Report, Department of Superintendence of the NEA* (1932):193-99.

_____. *Freedom, Culture, Social Planning, and Leadership.* Washington, DC: National Council of Education of the NEA, 1932, pp. 3-6.

_____. Introduction to *The Crisis of Capitalism in America,* by M. J. Brown. Translated by Winifred Ray. New York: John Day Co., 1932, pp. 7-15.

_____; Reed, Thomas H.; and Jones, Howard P. "Redrawing the Boundaries of Local Government." *Government Series Lecture,* no. 2 (Chicago: University of Chicago Press, 1932). 13 pp.

_____. "Secondary Education and the Social Problem." *School Executives Magazine* 51 (August 1932):499-501, 519-20.

_____. "The Soviet Planning System and the Five-Year Plan," and "Discussion of the Economic Systems of Facism, Communism, and Capitalism: First Conference." In *Bolshevism, Facism, and Capitalism: An Account of the Three Economic Systems,* pp. 1-54 and 202-27. By George S. Counts, Luigi Villari, Malcolm C. Rorty, and Newton D. Baker. New Haven: Published for the Institute of Politics by the Yale University Press, 1932.

_____. " 'Theses' and Report of a Discussion." *NEA Proceedings* 70 (1932):249-51.

_____. "Vision of a New Age Urged in Education." *New York Times,* 21 February 1932, sec. 3, p. 7.

1933

[_____.] *A Call to the Teachers of the Nation.* American Education Fellowship Committee on Social and Economic Problems. New York: John Day Co., 1933. 31 pp.

_____; Norton, John K.; and Simon, Robert E. "Reducing the School Budget." *National Municipal Review* 22 (August 1933):374-80, 388.

_____. "What Has Happened to the American Family?" *Columbia University Quarterly* 25 (December 1933):268-92.

1934

[_____, and Beard, Charles A.]. *Conclusions and Recommendations of the Commission.* Report of the Commission on the Social Studies. New York: Charles Scribner's Sons, 1934. 168 pp.

_____. "Financing the Social Frontier." *Social Frontier* 1 (November 1934):32.

_____. "Implications for Education and Teacher-Training." In *Problems in Teacher Training,* pp. 240-53. Compiled and edited by Alonzo F. Myers. *Eastern States Association of Professional Schools for Teachers Proceedings,* vol. 8. New York: Prentice-Hall, 1934.

[_____.] "Orientation." *Social Frontier* 1 (October 1934):3-5.

_____, et al. *The Social Foundations of Education.* New York: Charles
Scribner's Sons, 1934. 579 pp.

_____. "A Symptom of Revolt." Review of *A Primer for Tomorrow* by
Christian Gauss. *New Republic* 79 (8 August 1934):351.

1935

_____. "The Cultural Lag." Review of *Social Change and Education.*
Social Frontier 1 (March 1935):27-28.

_____. "Education and the Social Problem." *Southern Review* 1 (1935):
295-307.

_____. "Education in the Soviet Union." In *Exhibition of Education in
the Soviet Union*, p. 5. New York: American Museum of Natural
History, 1935.

_____. "Education in the U.S.S.R." *New Republic* 82 (13 February 1935):
8-11.

_____. "Large vs. Small Classes." *New York Times*, 26 May 1935, sec. 11,
p. 14.

_____; Kilpatrick, William H.; and Newlon, Jesse H. "The New Attack on
Freedom of Teaching." *Journal of the National Education Association* 24 (February 1935):51-52.

_____. "The Opportunity of the Social Studies Teacher." *Proceedings of
the Middle States Association of History Teachers* (1935):30-36.

_____. "The Plight of the Middle Class." Review of *The Crisis of the Mid-
dle Class* by Lewis Corey, *Social Frontier* 2 (Dec. 1955):89.

_____. "Presentday Reasons for Requiring a Longer Period of Pre-Service
Preparation for Teachers." In *The American Association of Teachers
Colleges, Fourteenth Yearbook*, pp. 89-96. Washington, DC: Na-
tional Education Association, 1935.

_____. "Presentday Reasons for Requiring a Longer Period of Pre-Service
Preparation for Teachers." *NEA Proceedings* 73 (1935):694-701.

_____. "Three Hundred Years of the Secondary School Curriculum." *Bul-
letin of the Department of Secondary-School Principals* 55 (March
1935):111-22.

1936

_____, et al. "Democracy and the Profession of Teaching." *NEA Proceed-
ings* 74 (1936):146-49.

_____. "Education in a Changing Society." *Educational Trends* 4 (August
1936):18-25.

_____, et al. "Jury-Panel Discussion of 1936 Yearbook." *NEA Proceed-
ings* 74 (1936):444-67.

_____. "The Opportunity of the Social Studies Teacher." *Social Studies*
27 (January 1936):6-11.

1937

_____. "Business in Education." In *Relations of Public Education and Private Enterprise*, pp. 1-8. New York: School of Education, Teachers College, Columbia University, 1937.

_____; Stevenson, Archibald E.; Stoddard, A. J.; Davis, Madeline F.; and Hall, Lolabel. *How Free Should Our Schools Be?* America's Town Meeting of the Air Series 2, no. 16 (4 March 1937). New York: American Book Company, 1937. 33 pp.

_____. "The Prospect of American Democracy." *NEA Proceedings* 75 (1937):502-14.

_____. "The Prospect of American Democracy." *American Association of School Administrators, Official Report* (1937):132-45.

1938

_____. "Business and Education." *Teachers College Record* 39 (April 1938):553-60.

_____. "A Program for American Education." *Educational Trends* 6 (October-November 1938):1-6.

_____. *The Prospects of American Democracy*. New York: John Day Co., 1938. 370 pp.

_____. "To Vitalize American Tradition." *Progressive Education* 15 (March 1938):245.

1939

_____. "An Address." In *Labor and Education in 1939*, pp. 19-20. American Federation of Labor, 1939.

_____. "AFL Reaffirms and Enlarges Its Faith in Education." *American Teacher* 24 (November 1939):5-6.

_____. "The Current Challenge to Our Democratic Heritage." *Progressive Education* 16 (February 1939):91-97.

_____. *Education and Democracy*. Chicago: American Federation of Teachers, 1939. 3 pp.

_____. "Is Our Union Controlled by Communists?" *American Teacher* 24 (December 1939):5-6.

_____. "Our Articles of Faith." *National Parent Teacher* 34 (October 1939):16-20.

_____. "Our Job for the Current Year." *American Teacher* 24 (October 1939):5-6.

_____. "The Promise of American Democracy." In *Democracy and the Curriculum*, pp. 187-225. Edited by Harold Rugg. Third Yearbook of John Dewey Society. New York: D. Appleton-Century Company, 1939.

_____. "Rally Around AFT Program: Acceptance Speech." *American Teacher* 24 (September 1939):1-2.

_____. "The School and the State in American Democracy." *NEA Proceedings* 76 (1939):178-80.

_____. *The Schools Can Teach Democracy*. New York: John Day Co., 1939. 32 pp.

_____. "Whose Twilight?" *Social Frontier* 5 (February 1939):135-40.

1940

_____. "AFL Generously Supports Teachers' Organizing Drive." *American Teacher* 25 (November 1940):5, 31.

_____. "AFT Must Launch Organization Drive." *American Teacher* 25 (September 1940):1.

_____. "America Faces a Fast-Changing World at War." *American Teacher* 25 (September 1940):9-10.

_____. "A Defense Decalogue for Educators." *School Review* 48 (October 1940):566-68.

_____. "Educators in This Crisis." *New Republic* 103 (26 August 1940): 268-69.

_____. "How Can We Achieve Unity?" *American Teacher* 24 (March 1940):5-6.

_____. "How They Are Voting." Letter to *New Republic* 103 (23 September 1940):412.

_____. "The National Income Must Be Increased." *American Teacher* 24 (April 1940):5-6.

_____, comp. "Perpetual Exclusion of Negroes from Democratic Rights." *American Teacher* 24 (January 1940):7-8.

_____. *Presidential Address*. Chicago: American Federation of Teachers, 1940.

_____. "A Sustaining Fund for Academic Freedom Cases." *American Teacher* 24 (February 1940):5-6.

_____. "Teaching of Patriotism." *American Teacher* 25 (October 1940):7.

_____. *Why I Joined*. Chicago: American Federation of Teachers, [1940]. 2 pp.

1941

_____. "The Action of the Council on the New York Situation." *American Teacher* 25 (February 1941):7.

_____. "A Challenge to AFT Members." *American Teacher* 26 (December 1941):30.

_____. "Communism, Fascism or Democracy." *American Teacher* 25 (May 1941):3-4. Abridged in *Congressional Record* 87:A4316-17.

_____. "Democracy As a Great Social Faith." *National Parent Teacher* 36 (September 1941):24-26.

[_____.] Educational Policies Commission. *The Education of Free Men in American Democracy*. Washington, DC: National Education Association, 1941. 115 pp.

_____; Smith, Stanton E.; and Axtelle, George E. "The Executive Council's Proposal to Save the AFT." *American Teacher* 25 (April 1941): 2, 4-17.

_____. "Introduction to Part III: Four Great Patterns of American Culture." In *Readings in the Foundation of Education*, vol. 1, pp. 299-32. Edited by Harold Rugg. New York: Teachers College, Columbia University, 1941.

_____. "Labor's Stake in a Victory." *Nation* 152 (22 March 1941): 360-63.

_____. "A Liberal Looks at Life." *Frontiers of Democracy* 7 (May 1941): 231-32.

_____. "NAM Investigates Textbooks." *American Teacher* 25 (January 1941):7.

_____. "Presidential Address." *District Teacher* 12 (October 1941): 5-8.

_____. "President's Annual Report." *American Teacher* 26 (October 1941):5-8. Abridged in *Congressional Record* 87:A2492.

_____, and Brameld, Theodore. "Relations with Public Education: Some Specific Issues and Proposals." In *Workers' Education in the United States*, pp. 249-77. Edited by Theodore Brameld. Fifth Yearbook of the John Dewey Society. New York: Harper and Row, 1941.

_____. "Report of Executive Council." *American Teacher* 25 (March 1941):4.

_____. "Welcome Home." *Guild Teacher* 6 (June 1941):2.

_____; Douglas, Paul; Baker, Frank E.; and Voorhis, Jerry. *Why I Belong to the American Federation of Teachers* (A.F.T. Pamphlet, 1941), 1 p.

1942

_____. "AFL's Program for the War." *American Teacher* 26 (January 1942):31.

_____. "The Challenge to the Secondary School." *American Association of School Administrators Proceedings* (1942):253-57.

_____. "The Coming Gary Convention." *American Teacher* 26 (May 1942):39.

_____. "Education for War and Peace." *American Teacher* 26 (February 1942):31.

_____. "Education in an Age of Decision." *Curriculum Journal* 13 (November 1942):303-7.

_____ et al. *Federal Aid and the Crisis in American Education*. Chicago: American Federation of Teachers [1942], 9 pp.

_____. "Lessons from Britain." *American Teacher* 26 (March 1942):31.

_____. "Retiring President's Report to the Gary Convention." *American Teacher* 27 (October 1942):5-8.

_____. "What We Fight For." *American Teacher* 26 (April 1942):31.

1943

_____, and Childs, John L. *America, Russia, and the Communist Party in the Postwar World*. New York: John Day Co., 1943. 92 pp.

_____. "Education for a New World" and "Needed New Patterns of Control." In *Mobilizing Educational Resources*, pp. 1-15 and 223-37. Edited by Ernest O. Melby. Sixth Yearbook of the John Dewey Society. New York: Harper and Bros., 1943.

_____. "Education and Wisdom." Review of *Liberal Education* by Mark Van Doren. *Nation* 157 (11 December 1943):706-8.

_____. "Must Not Let NRPB Be Killed by Congress." Letter to *American Teacher* 27 (May 1943):16.

1944

_____. "Education and Postwar America." *American Teacher* 28 (May 1944):9-12.

_____. "Education and Postwar America." *American Federationist* 51 (July 1944):24-26.

1945

_____. *Education and the Promise of America*. New York: The Macmillan Co., 1945. 157 pp.

_____. "Remaking the Russian Mind." *Asia and the Americas* 45 (October 1945):478-84.

_____. "Russians Still Get Marxist View of Us." *New York Times*, 7 October 1945, p. 24. Reprinted in *Congressional Record* 91: A4210-11.

_____. "To Overtake and Surpass America." *Asia and the Americas* 45 (November 1945):534-37.

1946

_____. "Browder is Disputed." *New York Times*, 15 September 1946, p. 7.

_____. "Can the Schools Build Democracy in Japan?" *American Teacher* 31 (November 1946):11-13.

_____. "Can the Schools Build Democracy in Japan?" *World Outlook* 36 (Whole Series) (September 1946):383-85.

_____. "Recent Changes in Soviet Education." *Educational Forum* 10 (May 1946):423-36.

_____. "Remaking the Russian Mind." *Education Digest* 12 (November 1946):10-14.

_____. "Russia Softens History." *Christian Science Monitor Weekly Magazine* (26 October 1946):5.

_____. "The Second World War in a Soviet High School History." *Social Education* 10 (December 1946):345-47.

_____. "Soviet Textbook Defends Axis Tie." *New York Times*, 25 August 1946), p. 21.

_____. "To Overtake and Surpass America." *Education Digest* 12 (December 1946):34-37.

_____. "Soviet Version of American History." *Public Opinion Quarterly* 10 (Fall 1946):321-28.

1947

_____. "Are the Soviets Modifying Marxian Doctrines?" *School and Society* 65 (4 January 1947):1-3.

_____, and Lodge, Nucia P., trans. *I Want To Be Like Stalin*. By Boris Petrovich Yesipov and N. K. Goncharov. Introduction by George S. Counts, pp. 1-33. New York: John Day Co., 1947. 150 pp.

_____. "The Second World War in a Soviet High School History." *Education Digest* 12 (February 1947):5-7.

_____. "Socio-Economic Forces in Teachers' Strikes." *Phi Delta Kappan* 28 (April 1947):350, 352.

_____. "Some Recent Tendencies in Soviet Education." *American Teacher* 32 (November 1947):16-19.

_____. "Soviet-American Understanding Through Education." In *Twenty-Sixth Yearbook of the American Association of Teachers Colleges* (1947):68-74.

1948

_____. "The Challenge of Soviet Education." *School Life* 30 (February 1948):18-19, 23-24.

_____. "A Memorable Occasion." *Teachers College Record* 49 (January 1948):265.

_____; Childs, John L.; and Reeves, Floyd W. *To Provide for the Common Defense*. Chicago: American Federation of Teachers, 1948. 10 pp.

1949

_____, and Lodge, Nucia P. *The Country of the Blind: The Soviet System of Mind Control*. Boston: Houghton-Mifflin Co., 1949. 378 pp.

_____. "Educate for Democracy." *Phi Delta Kappan* 30 (February 1949): 194-97.

_____. "The End of a Myth About Education and Democracy." *Vital Speeches* 15 (15 February 1949):266-69.

_____. "The Soviet System of Mind Control." I: "The Party of Lenin and Stalin" (15 July 1949); II: "The Resolutions of the Central Committee" (15 August 1949); III: "The Assault on Individuals" (15 September 1949); IV: "The Confession of a Scientist" (15 October 1949); V: "The Responses of the People" (15 November 1949); VI: "The Letter to Stalin" (15 December 1949). *Workers Education Bureau of America*, 1949.

1950

_____. "Meeting the Communist Challenge." *Elks Magazine* 28 (March 1950):4-5, 35-38.

[_____.] Educational Policies Commission. *Point Four and Education.* Washington, D.C.: National Education Association, 1950. 27 pp.

_____. "The Soviet Russia Formula." In *Leadership in American Education,* pp. 24-26. Edited by Alonzo G. Grace. *Proceedings of the Conference for Administrative Officers of Public and Private Schools* (1950).

_____. "The Soviet System of Mind Control." *Educational Forum* 14 (May 1950):389-98.

1951

_____. *American Education Through the Soviet Looking Glass.* New York: Bureau of Publications, Teachers College, Columbia University, 1951. 48 pp.

_____. "American Education Through the Soviet Looking Glass." *Teachers College Record* 52 (February 1951):297-309.

_____. "The Central Ideological Conflict of Our Time." *Educational Leadership* 9 (December 1951):143-49.

_____ et al. "Coverage of Rousset Trial." Letter to the Times. *New York Times,* 15 February 1951, p. 30.

_____. "Education for a World Society." In *Education for a World Society,* pp. 3-15. Edited by Christian O. Arndt and Samuel Everett. Eleventh Yearbook of the John Dewey Society. New York: Harper and Bros., 1951.

_____. Foreword to *The American Common School,* by Lawrence A. Cremin. New York: Bureau of Publications, Teachers College, Columbia University, 1951, pp. vii-viii.

_____. "Mind Control in the Soviet Union." *NEA Journal* 40 (January 1951):29-32.

_____. "The Need for a Great Education." *Teachers College Record* 53 (November 1951):77-88.

_____. "Should Communism Be Studied in Our Schools?" *School Executive* 70 (March 1951):60.

1952

_____. "Croce's Career." Letter to the Times. *New York Times,* 23 November 1952, sec. 4, p. 8.

_____. *Education and American Civilization.* New York: Bureau of Publications, Teachers College, Columbia University, 1952. 491 pp.

_____. "Education and Our American Values." Philadelphia: The Dropsite College for Hebrew and Cognate Learning, 1952, pp. 12-19.

_____. "The Soviet System of Mind Control." *Congressional Record* 98:A4417-20.

1953

_____. "Let's Enter the Twentieth Century." *American Unity* 12 (September-October 1953):3-5.

_____. "The Moral Foundations of American Civilization." *Fortieth Annual Schoolmen's Week Proceedings* 40 (Philadelphia: University of Pennsylvania Bulletin, 1953):188-94.

_____. "A Proposal for Improving the Quality of Instruction and Discipline in the Public School." *Progressive Education* 30 (February 1953): 123-26.

_____. "Russia As Asylum." Letter to the Times. *New York Times*, 8 February 1953, sec. 4, p. 8.

_____. "To Guard Civil Liberties." Letter to the Times. *New York Times*, 27 January 1953, p. 24.

1954

_____. "Charles Beard, the Public Man." In *Charles A. Beard: An Appraisal*, pp. 231-53. Edited by Howard K. Beale. University of Kentucky Press, 1954.

_____. *Decision Making and American Values in School Administration*. New York: Bureau of Publications, Teachers College, Columbia University, 1954. 90 pp.

_____. "Freedom of Teaching." *Vital Speeches* 20 (15 August 1954):659-61.

_____. *The Right to Make Mistakes*. New York: League for Industrial Democracy [1954]. 14 pp.

_____. "V.F.W. Action Criticized." Letter to the Times. *New York Times*, 30 January 1954, p. 16.

1956

_____. Foreword to *An Introduction to Education in American Society*, by Raymond E. Callahan. New York: Alfred A. Knopf, 1956, pp. v-viii. Also in 2d edition, 1960, pp. v-viii.

_____. "The Intangible Supports of Liberty." *Educational Forum* 20 (January 1956):133-40.

_____. Letter. *New Republic* 135 (2 July 1956):23.

1957

_____, assisted by Lodge, Nucia P. *The Challenge of Soviet Education*. New York: McGraw-Hill, 1957. 331 pp.

_____. "The Challenge of Soviet Education." *MacLeans* 70 (16 February 1957):10, 11, 28, 30, 32, 34-36.

_____. "Soviet Education and Soviet Power." *Teachers College Record* 58 (March 1957):293-300.

_____. "Soviet Education and Soviet Power." *Education Digest* 23 (September 1957):1-4.

1958

_____. "The Challenge of Soviet Education." *Social Education* 22 (April 1958):181-86.

_____. "Education and the Foundations of Liberty." *Teachers College Record* 59 (April 1958):403-10.

_____. "Education and the Foundations of Liberty." *Education Digest* 24 (September 1958):1-5.

_____. "Education and the Technological Revolution." *Teachers College Record* 59 (March 1958):309-18.

_____. "Meeting the Challenge of Soviet Education." *American Teacher Magazine* 43 (December 1958):7-8, 22.

_____. *Meeting the Soviet Challenge.* New York Liberal Party Pamphlet (April 1958). 15 pp.

_____. "A Rational Faith in Education." *Teachers College Record* 59 (February 1958):249-57.

_____. "The Spirit of American Education." *Teachers College Record* 59 (May 1958):450-59.

1959

_____. "A Hungarian Odyssey." Review of *Child of Communism*, by Ede Pfeiffer. *New Leader* 42 (18 May 1959):22-23.

_____. *Krushchev and the Central Committee Speak on Education.* Pittsburgh: University of Pittsburgh Press, 1959. 66 pp.

_____. "The Real Challenge of Soviet Education." *Educational Forum* 23 (March 1959):261-69.

_____. "The Real Challenge of Soviet Education." *Education Digest* 25 (September 1959):5-8.

1960

_____. "Education Is a Weapon." Review of *The Communist and the Schools* by Robert W. Iverson. *New Leader* 43 (11 April 1960):26-27.

_____. "Meeting the Challenge of Soviet Education." *Studies in Contemporary Educational Thought*, vol. 40, no. 11 (Emporia, KA: Kansas State Teachers College, 1960):37-41.

1961

_____. "The Closing of the Great Cycle," *Phi Delta Kappan* 42 (April 1961):[329].

1962

_____. *Education and the Foundations of Human Freedom*. Pittsburgh: University of Pittsburgh Press, 1962. 104 pp.

_____. "The Redirection of Public Education: A Frontier of the Sixties." In *Redirection of Public Education*, pp. 9-32. Edited by Francis T. Villemain. Toledo: College of Education, University of Toledo, 1962.

_____. Review of *Education and Professional Employment in the USSR*, by Nicholas DeWitt. *Slavic Review* 21 (September 1962):568-69.

1964

_____. Introduction to *Two Worlds*, by Casimer C. Gecys. Bronx, New York: Institute of Contemporary Russian Studies, Fordham University, 1964, pp. v-vii.

1965

_____. "Dare the Schools Build the Great Society?" *Phi Delta Kappan* 47 (September 1965):27-30.

1966

_____. "Education and Catastrophe." *Kappa Delta Pi Lectures* (Kent, Ohio: Kent State University, 1966):9-17.

_____. "Education and the American Way of Life: Yesterday, Today, and Tomorrow." *Kappa Delta Pi Lectures* (Kent, Ohio: Kent State University, 1966):19-28.

_____. "Where Are We?" *Educational Forum* 30 (May 1966):397-406.

1967

_____. "The Creation of the New Soviet Man." *School and Society* 95 (25 November 1967):438-44.

_____. "George S. Counts After 50 Years of College Teaching." Interviewed by John Paul Eddy. *Phi Delta Kappan* 48 (June 1967):504-9.

_____. Preface to *Nationalism in School Education in China*, by Chiu-Sam Tsang. 2d ed. Hong Kong: Progressive Education Publishers, 1967, pp. i-ii.

1968

_____. Foreword to *And Merely Teach*, by Arthur E. Lean. Carbondale and Edwardsville, IL: Southern Illinois University Press, 1968, pp. vii-ix. Also 2d ed., 1976, pp. xi-xiii.

_____. Review of *The Learning Society*, by Robert M. Hutchins. *United Teacher* (12 June 1968):14.

1969

_____. "Education for Tomorrow's World." *Daily Egyptian* (Carbondale, IL), 8 March 1969, p. 2.

_____. Foreword to *Personal Worries and Fears of the High School Seniors in Sangalore City: Mysore State*, by Kananur V. Chandrasekharaiah. Los Angeles: Cultural Exchange Center, 1969, p. i.

_____. Introduction to *Contemporary Soviet Education*, by Fred Ablin. White Plains, NY: International Arts and Science Press, 1969, pp. vii-xiii.

_____. "Introduction to the Octagon Edition." Introduction to *Russia's Educational Heritage*, by William H. E. Johnson. New York: Octagon Books, 1969, pp. vii-viii.

_____. "Should the Teacher Always Be Neutral?" *Phi Delta Kappan* 51 (December 1969):186-89.

_____. *S.I.U. Alumnus* 30 (March 1969):10.

_____. "A Turning Point in My Life." *Theory Into Practice* 8 (December 1969):300-1.

1970

_____. Foreword to *The Prospects for Democracy in India*, by Kalulal Shrimali. Carbondale, IL: Southern Illinois University Press, 1970, pp. ix-xi.

1971

_____. "A Humble Autobiography." In *Leaders in Education*, pp. 151-74. Edited by Robert J. Havighurst. *Seventieth Yearbook of the National Society for the Study of Education*, 70, pt. 2 (Chicago: N.S.S.E., 1971).

_____. "International, Intercultural, and Interracial Education." *Viewpoints* 47 (September 1971):1-18.

1972

_____. "A Rational Faith in Education." In *College of Education Newsletter*, Southern Illinois University, Carbondale 11 (December 1971-January 1972):1-6.

Index